MW00951153

WORKPLACE VIOLENCE PREVENTION

DTS™

(Defensive Tactics System)

Student Guide

Education, Prevention, & Mitigation for Violence in the Workplace

David Fowler

Founder and Author of
AVADE® Workplace Violence Training Programs

WORKPLACE VIOLENCE PREVENTION

DTS™ Student Guide

Disclaimer

Personal Safety Training Inc.
Telephone: (208) 691-7481
www.AVADEtraining.com
www.PersonalSafetyTraining.com

Also, by David Fowler

Violence In The Workplace, Violence In the Workplace II, Violence In the Workplace III,
Be Safe Not Sorry, To Serve and Protect, SURVIVE an Active Shooter

ACKNOWLEDGEMENTS

I would like to thank the many teachers, instructors, mentors, and friends that have helped make this program a reality. Without your help, inspiration, and invaluable knowledge, this wouldn't have been possible.
To all of you, I am eternally grateful.

I would also like to thank the thousands of individuals that I have worked with whose direct and indirect contribution to this program has made it possible for me to do what I feel on purpose to do.

Special thanks to the following individuals for their support and technical advice: Steve Baker, Jason Blessinger, Genelle Fowler, Patrick Gibney, Brian Goodwin, Jamie Lang, and Eduardo Montez.

I would also like to thank my family for their support; I love you all so much!

David Fowler
Founder, AVADE® Personal Safety Training & Workplace Violence Prevention Programs
President, Personal Safety Training, Inc.

The author and the publisher, Personal Safety Training, Inc., do not dictate policies or procedures for the use of any violence prevention, self-defense, or any physical intervention authorized for use by a department/agency or private individual. The suggestions/options disseminated in this book are simply that, suggestions or options. Each individual, department, or agency is responsible for developing their own "policies and procedures" regarding the use of violence prevention, self-defense, and physical intervention for their personnel and for themselves. Although every effort has been made for this book to be complete and accurate, it is impossible to predict, discuss or plan for every circumstance or situation which might arise in the course of defending yourself during any contact with a violent or aggressive person(s) or during a crime.

Every reader must always take into consideration his/her experience, physical abilities, professional responsibilities, agency and department procedures, and local, state, and federal legal requirements. With this in mind, each reader must evaluate the recommendations and techniques contained in this book and decide for himself (herself), which should be used, and under what circumstances. Each reader assumes the risk of loss, injury, and damages associated with this book and the use of the information obtained in it. The author and publisher, Personal Safety Training, Inc., cannot guarantee or warrant the legal, medical, tactical, or technical suggestions/options in this book.

ANY IMPLIED WARRANTIES ARE EXPRESSLY DISAVOWED.

CONTENTS

Introduction

In today's society, law enforcement, security, corrections, military, and protective services agencies realize that defensive tactics strategies, and techniques are essential for protecting themselves and the public that they serve. These agencies also understand that mitigating liability begins with proper training and education in defensive tactics strategies and techniques.

AVADE® DTS™

Training and **education** designed to **empower** officers, **increase awareness**, **knowledge**, **skills**, and **responses** with regard to Use of Force, Control and Restraint, and Self-Defense.

The AVADE® Defensive Tactics System™ is a training program designed for public safety officers to reduce the potential of injury and liability risk when lawfully defending themselves or controlling an aggressive individual. The tactics and techniques in this training curriculum are for incidents where the aggressor is physically resistive and unarmed.

This training manual for the AVADE® Defensive Tactics System™ provides training and education that is designed to empower officers, increase awareness, knowledge, skills, and actions with regard to the use of force, control and restraint, self-defense, and defending others with defensive tactics strategies and techniques.

This course stresses the importance of knowing your agency's policies and procedures in regard to using force and defending yourself or another person. The AVADE® Defensive Tactics System™ training is intended to give the trainee a basic understanding of self-defense, use of force, control and restraint, reasonable force, and basic legal definitions of force. Personal Safety Training Inc. makes no legal declaration, representation, or claim as to what force should be used or not used during self-defense, use of force incident, or assault incident or situation. Each trainee must take into consideration their ability, agency policies and procedures, and laws in the state and country in which they reside.

The techniques in this training course are uncomplicated for most individuals to learn and develop proficiency. Basic defensive tactics fundamentals are taught, followed by contact and cover positioning, escort strategies & techniques, control & decentralization, handcuffing techniques, defensive blocking techniques, personal defense skills & techniques, weapon retention techniques, and post-incident response and documentation procedures.

This course is modular-based and can be taught over a period of one year or less to achieve a certificate of competency. Or it can be taught in its entirety in an eight-hour basic course to achieve a certificate of competency.

AVADE® FIRST RULE OF TRAINING = SAFETY

▶ AVADE® Training Safety Rules

1 **SAFETY & WAIVER AGREEMENT**
Each individual trained **MUST** complete the **Student Registration & Recertification Form**. The instructor will advise the student how to fill it out and answer any questions pertaining to it.

2 **WEAPONS FREE ENVIRONMENT**
NO WEAPONS are allowed anywhere in the training area. Instructor will advise participants in proper procedures in securing weapons and ammunition. Follow agency policy and procedures.

3 **REMOVE JEWELRY, ETC.**
The following should not be worn during a class which involves hands-on training: all jewelry with sharp edges, pins or raised surfaces, or jewelry that encircles the neck.

4 **NO HORSEPLAY RULE**
Any participant who displays a disregard for **SAFETY** to anyone in class will be asked to leave the class. Please practice only the technique currently being taught. **DO NOT PRACTICE UNAUTHORIZED TECHNIQUES.**

5 **PAT OUT RULE** (USED FOR PARTNER TECHNIQUES)
Upon hearing/feeling/seeing the "**PAT**," your partner applying the technique will immediately release the pressure of the technique to reduce discomfort/pain. The technique will be immediately and totally released on instructions from the instructor or when a safety monitor says "**RELEASE,**" "**STOP,**" or words similar to them.

6 **BE A GOOD "DEFENDER" AND A GOOD "AGGRESSOR"**
Essentially this means working together with your partner when practicing the techniques. Without cooperation while practicing self-defense or defensive control tactics techniques, time is wasted and injury potential is increased.

7 **PRACTICE TECHNIQUES SLOWLY AT FIRST**
Gain balance and correctness slowly before practicing for speed. Proceed at the pace directed by your trainer.

8 **CHECK EQUIPMENT FOR ADDED SAFETY**
The instructor will check **ALL** equipment used during the training to ensure proper function, working order and safety.

9 **ADVISE INSTRUCTOR OF ANY PRE-EXISTING INJURIES**
Any injury or condition that could be further injured or aggravated should be brought to the **immediate attention** of your instructor, and your partner, prior to participating in any hands-on training.

10 **ADVISE INSTRUCTOR OF ANY INJURY DURING CLASS**
Any injury, regardless of what it is, **needs to be reported** to the primary instructor.

11 **SAFETY IS EVERYONE'S RESPONSIBILITY!**
Safety is everyone's responsibility and everyone is empowered to **immediately report** or **YELL OUT** any safety violation.

12 **TRAINING HAZARDS**
Always keep any items or training equipment and batons off the floor/ground and out of the way when not in use.

13 **SAFETY MARKINGS**
Colored wrist bands or blue tape marking is a visual aid for pre-existing injury. Use **CAUTION**.

14 **LEAVING TRAINING AREA**
If you must leave the training area for any reason, please **advise your instructor** prior to doing so.

Education, Prevention, and Mitigation for *Violence in the Workplace*

© Personal Safety Training Inc. | AVADE® Training

Modular Based Training

The AVADE® Defensive Tactics System™ Training is a modular-based training program that can be taught in an eight-hour basic course or presented modularly during roll call, safety, or departmental meetings throughout a 12-month period.

AVADE® Defensive Tactics System™ Modules

1. **USE OF FORCE & SELF-DEFENSE**

2. **DEFENSIVE TACTICS FUNDAMENTALS**

3. **CONTACT & COVER TEAM POSITIONING**

4. **ESCORT STRATEGIES & TECHNIQUES**

5. **CONTROL & DECENTRALIZATION**

6. **HANDCUFFING TECHNIQUES**

7. **DEFENSIVE BLOCKING TECHNIQUES**

8. **PERSONAL DEFENSIVE TECHNIQUES**

9. **WEAPON RETENTION TECHNIQUES**

10. **POST-INCIDENT RESPONSE & DOCUMENTATION**

Modules & Objectives

1 — **USE OF FORCE & SELF-DEFENSE**

Mitigate liability risk through proper documentation & the understanding of **Use of Force** & **defense** of **one's self** or **others**.

2 — **DEFENSIVE TACTICS FUNDAMENTALS**

Provide proper **knowledge** & **awareness** of **Defensive Tactics Fundamentals** & techniques.

3 — **CONTACT & COVER TEAM POSITIONING**

Increase **awareness** & **understanding** of proper positioning with the use of **Contact & Cover Team Positioning** strategies.

4 — **ESCORT STRATEGIES & TECHNIQUES**

Provide proper **knowledge** & **awareness** of how to **effectively** & **safely** escort an individual with one or more persons.

5 — **CONTROL & DECENTRALIZATION**

Reduce the potential for **injury** & **assault** through proper **understanding** of **Control & Decentralization** when dealing with physically aggressive individuals.

6 — **HANDCUFFING TECHNIQUES**

Teach effective methods for handcuffing individuals in a **standing, kneeling,** or **prone** position.

Modules & Objectives

7 — DEFENSIVE BLOCKING TECHNIQUES

Provide **defensive blocking techniques** from **attacks** to various areas of the body.

8 — PERSONAL DEFENSE TECHNIQUES

Provide **defensive intervention** skills & techniques to **counter attacks** and bring an aggressive individual under **control**.

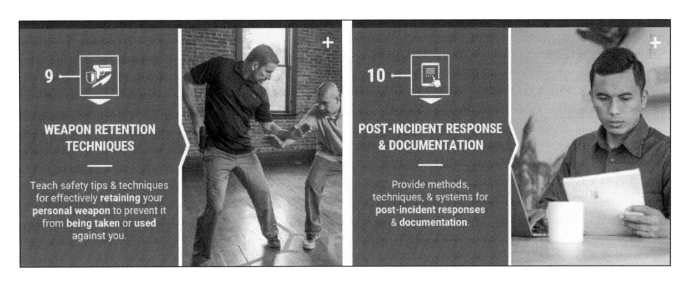

9 — WEAPON RETENTION TECHNIQUES

Teach safety tips & techniques for effectively **retaining** your **personal weapon** to prevent it from **being taken** or **used** against you.

10 — POST-INCIDENT RESPONSE & DOCUMENTATION

Provide methods, techniques, & systems for **post-incident responses** & **documentation**.

Module 1: Use of Force & Self-Defense

Any use of force or self-defense intervention must be reasonable and legally justified.

Awareness of "LIABILITY RISK"

When any force is used, the officer MUST take into consideration their ability, agency policies and procedures, and laws in the state and country in which they reside.

Unauthorized or inappropriate use of force or defense may expose the officer and/or agency to criminal and/or civil liability.

Personal Safety Training Inc. does not dictate policies or procedures for arrest, detention, control, and restraint, self-defense, use of force, or any physical intervention authorized for use by a department/agency or private individual. The suggestions, options, and techniques disseminated during this training program are simply that, suggestions, options, and techniques. Each individual, department, or agency is responsible for developing their own "policies and procedures" regarding the use of force, self-defense, physical intervention, physical restraints, physical control, arrest, and detention for their personnel.

Special Note for Healthcare Agencies: **Center for Medicaid Services**

- AVADE® training aligns with the Center for Medicaid Services (CMS) COP §482.13(e)(2) Restraint or seclusion may only be used when less restrictive interventions have been determined to be ineffective to protect the patient, a staff member, or others from harm.

- Any intervention other than verbal De-Escalation should only be used when it "is used for the management of violent or self-destructive behavior that jeopardizes the immediate physical safety of the patient, a staff member, or others," as defined by CMS.

▸ **PSTI** Legal Disclaimer

Personal Safety Training Inc. makes **no legal declaration, representation**, or **claim** as to what force should be used or not used during a **self-defense situation, assault situation**, or **use of force incident**.

What is Self-Defense?

Self-defense is the right to use **reasonable force** to **protect oneself or members of one's staff/family from bodily harm** from the attack of an aggressor if you have reason to believe that you or they are in **danger**.

Self-defense must always be your last resort. When it is used, the force used must be considered "reasonable,"; e.g., striking someone who yells an obscenity at you is not considered "reasonable force."

The best self-defense is to avoid the situation and get away. If avoidance and escape are not possible, a reasonable defense would be lawful as a last resort. You have the right to defend yourself; however, **any use of self-defense must follow any agency policy and procedure**, as well as state and federal law.

The following information will provide a general understanding of what self-defense and use of force are, how you can legally protect yourself against assault, as well as the risk of liability associated with any type of self-defense or force.

This module will give you a basic understanding of self-defense, assault, reasonable force and basic legal definitions of force. Personal Safety Training Inc. makes no legal declaration, representation or claim as to what force should be used or not used during a self-defense or assault incident or situation. Each individual must take into consideration their ability, agency policies and procedures, and laws in the state and country in which they reside.

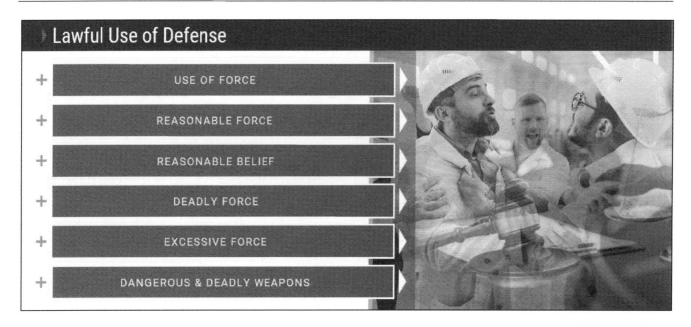

Lawful Use of Defense

+ USE OF FORCE
+ REASONABLE FORCE
+ REASONABLE BELIEF
+ DEADLY FORCE
+ EXCESSIVE FORCE
+ DANGEROUS & DEADLY WEAPONS

Use-of-Force

A term that describes the right of an individual or authority to settle conflicts or prevent certain actions by applying measures to either:

1. Dissuade another party from a particular course of action…or

2. Physically intervene to stop or control them.

Reasonable Force

- The degree of force which is not excessive and is appropriate in protecting one's self or one's property.

- When such force is used, a person is justified and is not criminally liable nor liable in tort. (A tort is an act that damages someone in some way and for which the injured person may sue the wrongdoer for damages.)

Reasonable Belief

The facts or circumstances that an individual knows, or should know, are such as to cause an ordinary and prudent person to act or think in a similar way under similar circumstances.

Deadly Force

Force that is likely or intended to cause death or great bodily harm. Deadly force may be reasonable or unreasonable, depending on the circumstances.

Excessive Force

That amount of force which is beyond the need and circumstances of the particular event, or which is not justified in the light of all the circumstances, for instance, in the case of deadly force to protect property as contrasted with protecting life.

Dangerous & Deadly Weapons

"Dangerous Weapon" is a device or instrument which, in the manner it is used, or intended to be used, is calculated or likely to produce death or great bodily harm.

"Deadly Weapons" includes any firearm, whether loaded or unloaded or a device designed as a weapon and capable of producing death or great bodily harm.

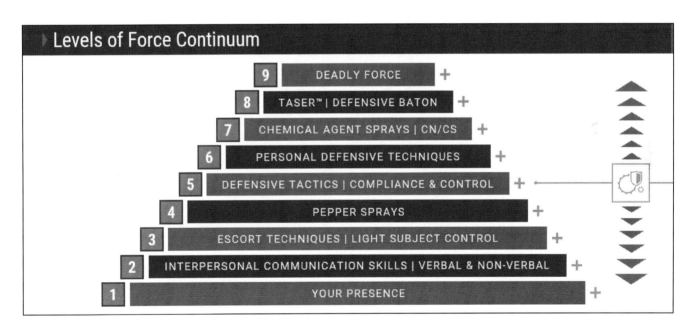

The use of force continuum is a standard that provides law enforcement officials & security personnel (such as police officers, probation officers, or corrections officers) with guidelines as to how much force may be used against a resisting subject in a given situation. In certain ways, it is similar to the military rules of engagement. The purpose of these models is to clarify, for both officers and citizens, the complex subject of the use of force by law officers.

Although various criminal justice agencies have developed different models of the continuum, there is no universal standard model.

The first examples of the use of force continua were developed in the 1980s and early 1990s. Early models were depicted in various formats, including graphs, semicircular "gauges," and linear progressions.

Most often, the models are presented in a "stair-step" fashion, with each level of force matched by a corresponding level of subject resistance, although it is generally noted that an officer need not progress through each level before reaching the final level of force. These progressions rest on the premise that officers should escalate and de-escalate their level of force in response to the subject's actions.

Although the use of force continuum is used primarily as a training tool for law officers, it is also valuable with civilians, such as in criminal trials or hearings by police review boards. In particular, a graphical representation of a use-of-force continuum is useful to a jury when deciding whether an officer's use of force was reasonable.

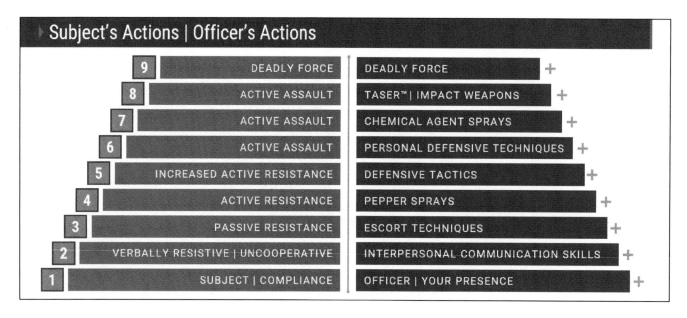

Agency Policies and Procedures

What are YOUR policies and procedures for the use of force and self-defense?

_____

_____

_____

Officers should have a strong understanding of their agency policies and procedures regarding the use of force and self-defense.

_____

_____

_____

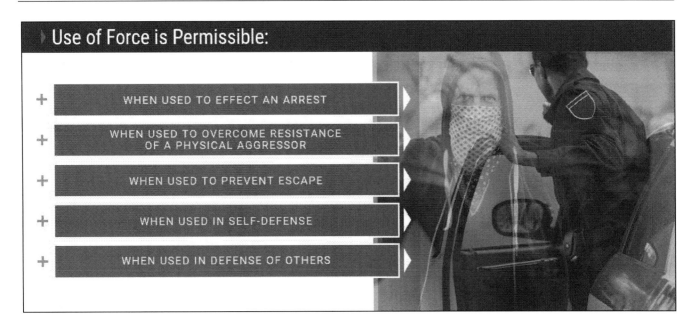

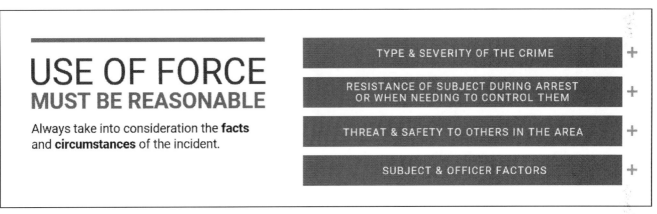

Every person must take into consideration their moral, legal, and ethical beliefs and rights and understandings when using any type of force to defend themselves or others. Personal Safety Training Inc. makes no legal declaration, representation or claim as to what force should be used or not used during a self-defense/assault incident or situation. Each individual must take into consideration their ability, agency policies and procedures and laws in their state and/or country.

_____

_____

_____

_____

_____

_____

_____

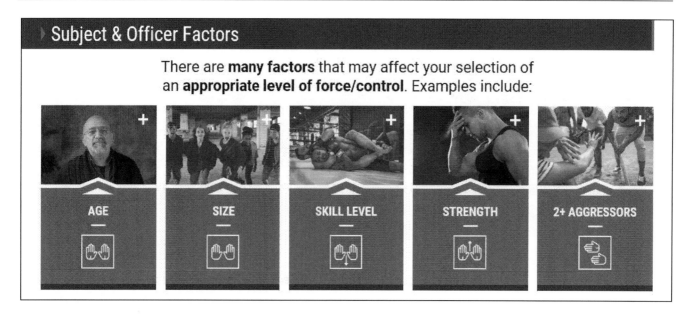

Age

In dealing with a subject who is agile, younger, faster, stronger, and has more stamina, an older officer may have to use more force/control. In contrast, a younger officer would use less control/force on an older person.

Size

In dealing with a larger subject, a smaller officer may need to use more force to control the subject. A larger officer would obviously use less force to control a subject who is smaller.

Skill Level

In dealing with a subject who is skilled in mixed martial arts or an expert in karate, it may be more difficult to control them based on their skill level. An officer who is skilled in defensive tactics may only need to use a minimum of force (with proper technique) to control a subject. An officer without current training and experience may need to use more force to control a subject.

Relative Strength

The different body compositions of males and females may be a factor in controlling a member of the opposite gender. Females typically have less torso strength than their male counterparts. A male officer may have to use less force to control a female subject. Whereas a female officer may need to use more force to control a male subject.

Multiple Aggressors

An officer who is being physically attacked by multiple aggressors is at a disadvantage. Even a highly skilled officer in defensive tactics is likely to be harmed in a situation such as this. In order to survive multiple aggressor attacks, higher levels of force may be necessary.

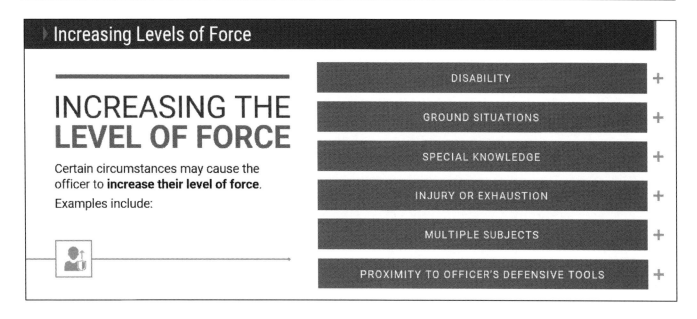

Increasing Levels of Force

INCREASING THE LEVEL OF FORCE

Certain circumstances may cause the officer to **increase their level of force**. Examples include:

- DISABILITY +
- GROUND SITUATIONS +
- SPECIAL KNOWLEDGE +
- INJURY OR EXHAUSTION +
- MULTIPLE SUBJECTS +
- PROXIMITY TO OFFICER'S DEFENSIVE TOOLS +

Disability: Officers who are disabled may find it necessary to increase the level of force to control a subject or to defend against an attack.

Ground Situations: If you are on the ground with a subject and you do not have control of them, you are at a disadvantage. Officers face a high risk of injury when not in control of a subject on the ground. You are also at a high risk of danger if you are on the ground and the subject is standing. Today, the popularity of mixed martial arts (MMA) can be a real threat to officers. The common vernacular with MMA is "the ground and pound." Officers must realize this and know that an increased level of force may be needed to survive a ground situation.

Special Knowledge: When an officer has encountered a subject with which they have had previous contact and knows the person's potential for combat or that they are prone to carrying weapons. The officer may need to approach the situation with the intent to increase the force rapidly if needed. Special knowledge may include martial arts background, propensity for using/carrying weapons, arrests, etc.

Injury or Exhaustion: If an officer is injured during a situation, the officer may need to increase the level of force to end the situation or bring it under control. Exhaustion is also an important factor. Having to physically control an individual for a prolonged length of time will rapidly fatigue an officer. An increased level of force may be needed to end the situation.

Proximity to the Officer's Defensive Tools: When an officer's defensive tool is taken from them, injury and even death may be imminent. Officers may need to escalate rapidly through the levels of force to survive this type of situation. The defensive tools that can be taken and used against an officer may include the following: firearms, chemical sprays, electronic stunning devices, impact weapons, etc.

Vulnerable Areas of the Body

Knowledge of **Self-Defense Tactics** is very important. Just as important is how and when you would utilize your **Self-Defense Tactics** skills **if** and **when** necessary.

Without this knowledge and understanding, your interventions could be ineffective or expose you to **unnecessary liability risk**.

The "**Vulnerable Areas**" of the body diagram denote **Lower**, **Medium**, and **High-Risk** Target Areas.

An individual **MUST ALWAYS** consider their policies and procedures, as well as State and Federal Laws, when using **force** or **self-defense** interventions.

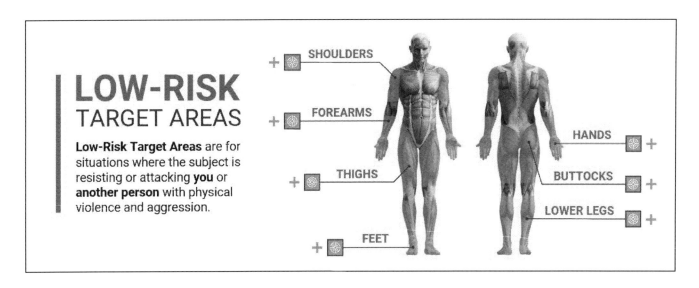

- The subject's body would be considered low risk for the application of blocks and restraint techniques (excluding the Head, Neck, Groin, and Spine).

- The level of resultant trauma to these areas tends to be minimal or temporary, yet exceptions may occur.

- An individual/agency MUST always consider their policies and procedures, state and federal laws when using any force or self-defense interventions.

Vulnerable Areas of the Body

Knowledge of **Self-Defense Tactics** is very important. Just as important is how and when you would utilize your **Self-Defense Tactics** skills **if** and **when** necessary.

Without this knowledge and understanding, your interventions could be ineffective or expose you to **unnecessary liability risk**.

The "**Vulnerable Areas**" of the body diagram denote **Lower**, **Medium**, and **High-Risk** Target Areas.

An individual **MUST ALWAYS** consider their policies and procedures, as well as State and Federal Laws, when using **force** or **self-defense** interventions.

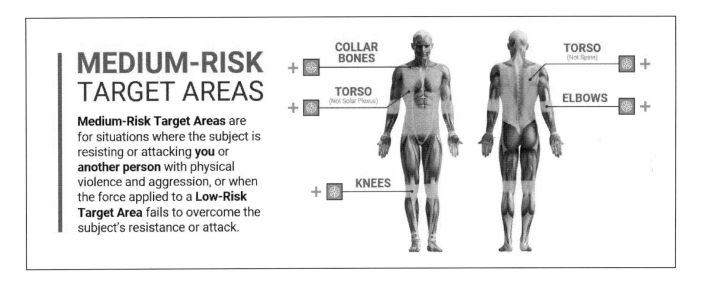

- Medium Risk Targets are areas of the human body that include joints and areas that are in close proximity to a High-Risk Target Area. The risk of potential injury is increased.

- The level of resultant trauma to these areas tends to be moderate to serious. Injury may last for longer periods of time or may be temporary.

- An individual/agency MUST always consider their policies and procedures, state and federal laws when using any force or self-defense interventions.

Vulnerable Areas of the Body

Knowledge of **Self-Defense Tactics** is very important. Just as important is how and when you would utilize your **Self-Defense Tactics** skills **if** and **when** necessary.

Without this knowledge and understanding, your interventions could be ineffective or expose you to **unnecessary liability risk**.

The "**Vulnerable Areas**" of the body diagram denote **Lower**, **Medium**, and **High-Risk** Target Areas.

An individual **MUST ALWAYS** consider their policies and procedures, as well as State and Federal Laws, when using **force** or **self-defense** interventions.

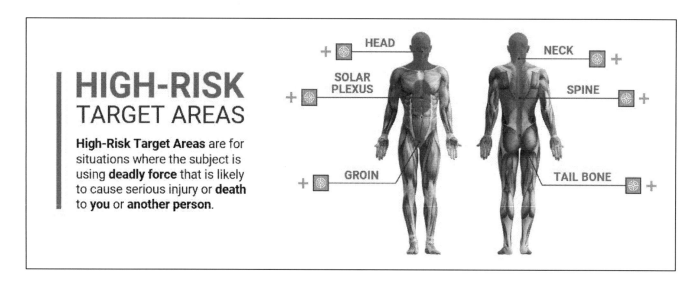

HIGH-RISK TARGET AREAS

High-Risk Target Areas are for situations where the subject is using **deadly force** that is likely to cause serious injury or **death** to **you** or **another person**.

HEAD — NECK — SOLAR PLEXUS — SPINE — GROIN — TAIL BONE

- Force-directed to High-Risk Target Areas may cause a greater risk of injury to the subject. Officers must be justified and reasonable in using deadly force against a subject.

- The level of resultant trauma to these areas tends to be serious and/or long-lasting. Injury to the subject may include serious bodily injury, unconsciousness, shock, or death.

- An individual/agency MUST always consider their policies and procedures, state and federal laws when using any force or self-defense interventions.

Module 2: Defensive Tactics Fundamentals

The defensive tactics fundamentals are the foundation of the Defense Tactics System™ training program. Without proper understanding and execution of the fundamentals, the techniques will be ineffective and useless.

Fundamentals

Fun·da·men·tal (from the Latin medieval: fundāmentālis: late Middle English)

—Synonyms 1. Indispensable, primary.

–adjective 1. Serving as, or being an essential part of, a foundation or basis; basic; underlying: fundamental principles; the fundamental structure.

2. Of, pertaining to, or affecting the foundation or basis: a fundamental revision.

3. Being an original or primary source: a fundamental idea.

–noun 1. A basic principle, rule, law, or the like, that serves as the groundwork of a system; essential part: to master the fundamentals of a trade.

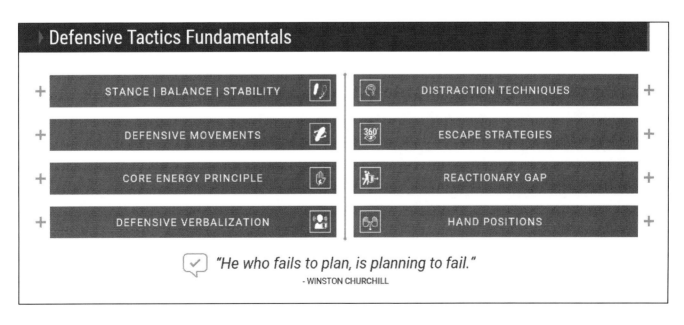

Defensive Tactics Fundamentals

STANCE | BALANCE | STABILITY	DISTRACTION TECHNIQUES
DEFENSIVE MOVEMENTS	ESCAPE STRATEGIES
CORE ENERGY PRINCIPLE	REACTIONARY GAP
DEFENSIVE VERBALIZATION	HAND POSITIONS

"He who fails to plan, is planning to fail."
- WINSTON CHURCHILL

Stance | Balance | Stability | Bladed Defensive Stance

The Bladed (defensive) Stance

All techniques in the defense tactics training are performed from the bladed stance.

Objective—Demonstrate how to correctly position your body to protect your vulnerable line and maintain stance, balance, and stability.

Performance—Bladed Stance

Face the clock (diagram on PowerPoint or imagine a clock in front of you) with your feet shoulder-width apart.

1. Step straight back with either left or right foot. Usually, individuals prefer to have their dominant foot to the rear.

2. If you step back with your right foot, turn your feet and body to the one o'clock position.

3. If you step back with your left foot, turn your feet and body to the eleven o'clock position.

4. Keep your weight equal on both feet and your knees slightly bent.

Performance Stability Test (Bladed Stance)

1. Partner exercise (A & B)

2. Partner A places his/her feet together. Partner B gently pushes partner A to the front, back, left side, and right side. Reverse roles.

3. Partner A stands with his/her feet should width apart. Partner B gently pushes partner A to the front, back, left side, and right side. Reverse roles.

4. Partner A now assumes the bladed stance. Partner B gently pushes partner A to the front, back, left side, and right side. Reverse roles.

The Bladed Stance protects your "Vulnerable Line" away from the subject.

ON TARGET TRAINING

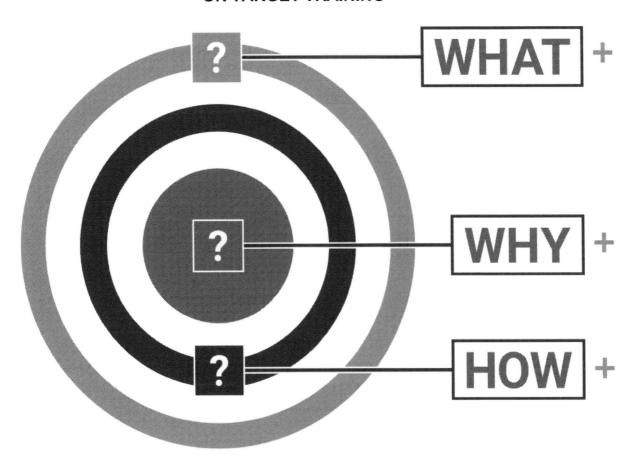

The WHAT describes a technique or tactic.
The first step in teaching a hands-on technique is to explain what the technique is by the name of it. For example, we will be learning about defensive movement, and the first defensive movement technique is forward shuffle.

While the HOW is the manner or method, the technique or tactic is performed.
The second step in teaching a hands-on technique is to explain and demonstrate how to do it. This step should be done a couple of times so that students can see it fully and completely.

And most importantly is the WHY. It's the purpose, reason, intention, justification, or motive of a technique or tactic.
The third step and most important step in teaching hands-on techniques is to explain why the technique is done a certain way and why you should have this technique in your arsenal of defenses. Without this understanding, the student is not bought into believing that the technique is needed or effective.

To really understand a technique or tactic, you must know the WHY (Bullseye).

Defensive Movements: Forward Shuffle

Forward movement is used to engage a subject for control or defense.

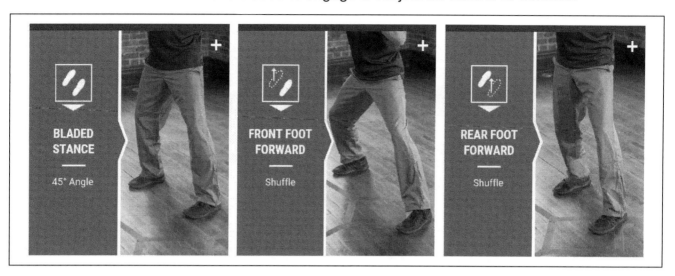

Forward Shuffle

This Defensive movement involves being able to move forward while maintaining balance and stability. All defensive tactics techniques are enhanced with defensive movement.

Objective—Demonstrate how to move forward correctly.

Performance—Forward Movement

1. Assume the bladed stance.

2. Take a short step forward with your front foot (shuffle).

3. Follow up with a short step forward using your rear foot.

4. Continue forward, using forward shuffling movement.

Caution: If the feet come together, balance and stability are compromised (common mistake).

The rule of defensive movement is: The foot that is closest to the direction you want to go always moves first.

Defensive Movements: Rear Shuffle

Rear movement is used to disengage from an aggressor.

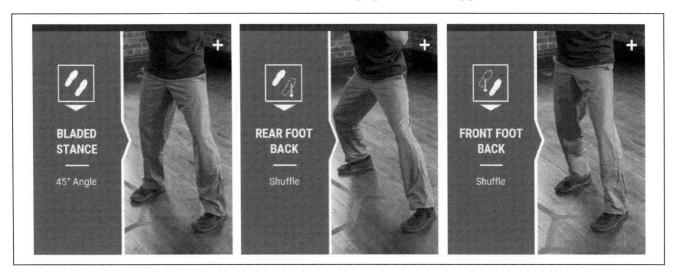

Rear Shuffle

This Defensive movement involves being able to move to the rear (backward) while maintaining balance and stability. All defensive tactics techniques are enhanced with defensive movement.

Objective—Demonstrate how to correctly move to the rear.

Performance—Rear Movement

1. Assume the bladed stance.

2. Take a short step back with the rear foot (shuffle).

3. Follow up with a short step back using your front foot.

4. Continue backward using the rear shuffling movement.

Caution: If the feet come together, balance and stability are compromised (common mistake).

Caution: Backpedaling is another common mistake.

Caution: Obstacles in your environment.

The rule of defensive movement is: The foot that is closest to the direction you want to go always moves first.

Defensive Movements: Side to Side Shuffle
Side-to-side movement is used to avoid an attack from an aggressor.

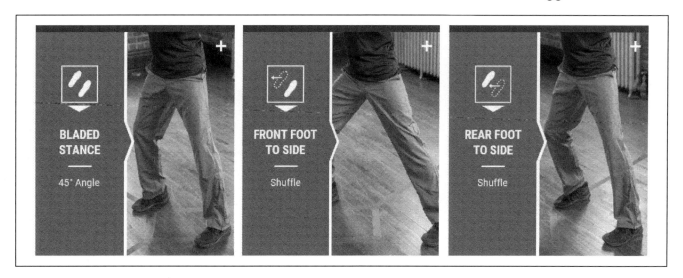

Side to Side Shuffle

This Defensive movement involves being able to move side to side while maintaining balance and stability. All defensive tactics techniques are enhanced with defensive movement.

Objective—Demonstrate how to correctly move side to side

Performance—Side-to-Side Movement

1. Assume the bladed stance.

2. Take a short step to the right using your right foot.

3. Follow up with a short step to the right using your left foot.

4. Take a short step to the left using your left.

5. Follow up with a short step to the left using your right foot.

Caution: If the feet come together, balance and stability are compromised (common mistake).

Caution: Crossing feet up is another common mistake.

Caution: Obstacles in your environment.

The rule of defensive movement is: The foot that is closest to the direction you want to go always moves first.

Defensive Movements: Forward and Rear Pivoting

Pivoting is used to reposition or to enhance your energy when using personal defensive techniques or defensive control tactics.

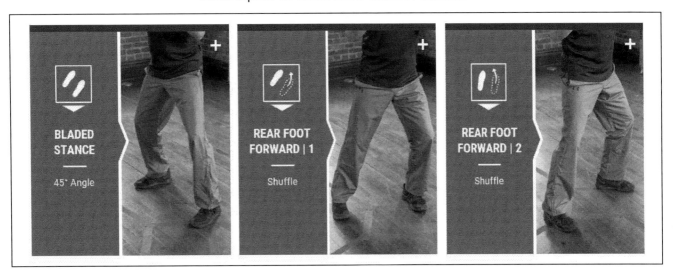

Forward & Rear Pivoting

This Defensive movement involves being able to pivot forward or back while maintaining balance and stability. All defensive tactics techniques are enhanced with defensive movement.

Objective—Demonstrate how to correctly pivot forward and backward.

Performance—Pivoting (forward and back)

1. Assume the bladed stance.

2. Take an arcing step forward with your rear foot (forward pivot).

3. Take an arcing step backward with your front foot (rear pivot).

4. When pivoting forward or backward, always remain balanced and stable.

5. Pivots can be small movements or up to a 360-degree pivot.

Caution: If the feet come together, balance and stability are compromised (common mistake).

Caution: Crossing feet up is another common mistake.

Caution: Obstacles in your environment.

Robot Exercise (The Best Self-Defense Technique!)

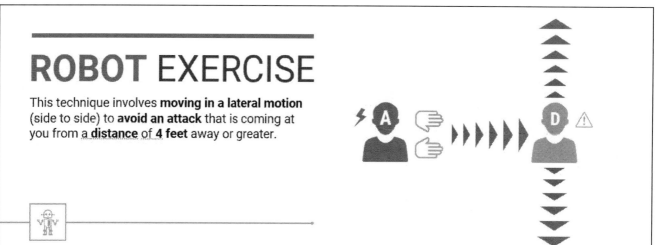

Defensive Movement Robot Exercise

The robot exercise involves being able to move in a lateral motion (side to side) to avoid an attack that is coming at you from a distance of 4' away or greater.

Objective—Demonstrate how to correctively avoid a forward attack by moving out of the way.

Performance—Robot Exercise

1. The defender assumes a bladed defensive stance.

2. From 4-6" away, the attacker places hands out directly toward the defender.

3. The attacker moves forward toward the defender, attempting to gently touch either shoulder of the defender.

4. The defender waits for the last moment to move to either side, away from the attack.

5. Using sounds and/or movements will assist the defender in distracting the attacker.

6. Once out of the attack zone, the defender can proceed to keep moving away from the attacker.

Caution: Do not move too late!

Caution: Do not move too soon, or the attacker will have time to adjust (reaction time) and follow/track you.

Caution: Crossing feet up is another common mistake.

Caution: Beware of obstacles in your environment.

Core Energy Principle

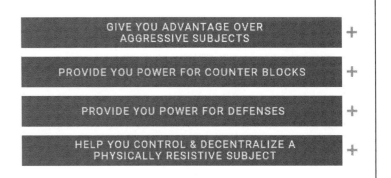

CORE ENERGY

Energy and **power** are generated and developed from the **core** of the human body, even though a lot of emphasis is placed on the body's extremities.

The **Core Energy Principle** will:

- GIVE YOU ADVANTAGE OVER AGGRESSIVE SUBJECTS +
- PROVIDE YOU POWER FOR COUNTER BLOCKS +
- PROVIDE YOU POWER FOR DEFENSES +
- HELP YOU CONTROL & DECENTRALIZE A PHYSICALLY RESISTIVE SUBJECT +

INEFFICIENT CORE ENERGY

Partner A faces Partner B with their **elbows away** from their core.

Partner A pushes Partner B back by pushing at their **shoulders**.

Reverse Roles

EFFICIENT CORE ENERGY

Partner A faces Partner B with their **elbows down** towards their core.

Partner A pushes Partner B back by pushing at their **shoulders**.

Reverse Roles

Core Energy

Our central and most essential part of our strength and power is our core energy. Without core energy, we rely on our extremities, which are not as strong as our central core. All defensive tactics techniques utilize this essential principle.

Objective—Demonstrate how to correctly use your core energy.

Performance—Core Energy

1. Partner exercise (A & B)

2. Partner A faces partner B with his/her elbows away from their core.

3. Partner B moves forward toward partner A. Partner A pushes partner B back by pushing at their shoulders. How did it go? Reverse roles.

4. Partner A again faces partner B with his/her elbows down towards their core. Partner B moves forward toward partner A. Partner A pushes partner B back by pushing at their shoulders. How did it go? Reverse roles

Defensive Verbalization

During **ALL** defenses use **loud** and **repetitive**
Defensive Verbalizations

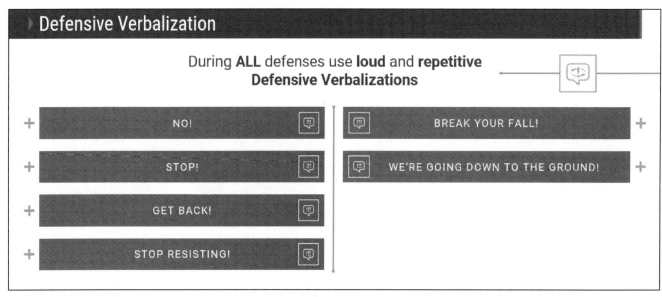

- NO!
- STOP!
- GET BACK!
- STOP RESISTING!
- BREAK YOUR FALL!
- WE'RE GOING DOWN TO THE GROUND!

Defensive Verbalization | Why?

1. Creates **witnesses**
2. Establishes **authority**
3. Keeps you **breathing**
4. May be used as a **distraction**
5. **Alerts others** of a confrontation
6. Provides **direction** to the aggressor
7. Mitigates **liability risk** | You & Agency

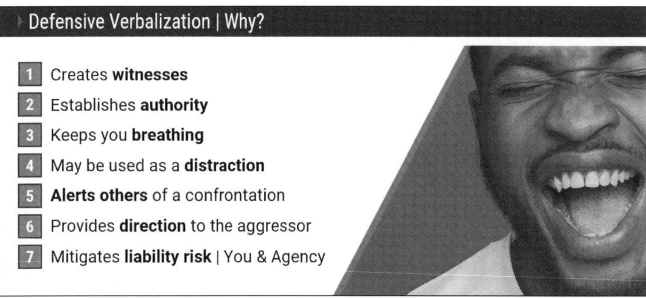

The Art of Distraction

A process by which we buy **valuable time** to **escape**, **defend**, or **control**.
Distractions have been used since ancient times. A **tactical advantage**!

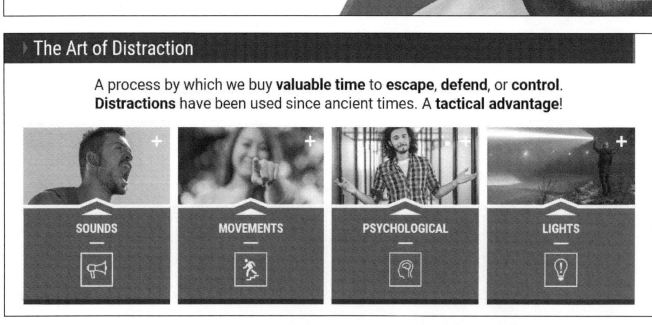

| SOUNDS | MOVEMENTS | PSYCHOLOGICAL | LIGHTS |

- **Distractions** are the process by which we **buy** valuable **time** to Escape, Defend, or Control.

- **Distractions affect** the **senses**, which take time for the mind to process the new information.

- **Distractions** have been used since ancient times. A **valuable advantage**!

Sounds – Movements – Psychological – Lights

- **Sounds:** Using a loud scream or yell can cause a momentary delay.

- **Movements:** Using your hands, eyes, and body can distract & cause a momentary delay.

- **Psychological:** Asking a question that is out of the ordinary can cause a mental delay.

- **Lights:** Flashlights, the sun, emergency lights, etc., can cause a delay.

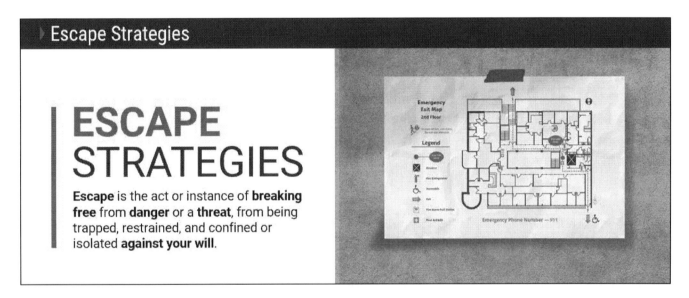

Escape Strategies

ESCAPE STRATEGIES

Escape is the act or instance of **breaking free** from **danger** or a **threat**, from being trapped, restrained, and confined or isolated **against your will**.

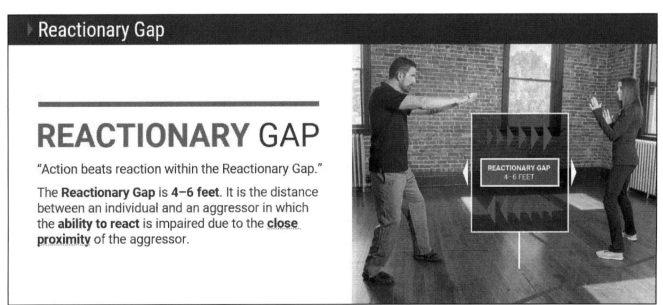

Reactionary Gap

REACTIONARY GAP

"Action beats reaction within the Reactionary Gap."

The **Reactionary Gap** is **4–6 feet**. It is the distance between an individual and an aggressor in which the **ability to react** is impaired due to the **close proximity** of the aggressor.

Hands

The hands have been the most important tools in human evolution. There are more connections between the brain and the hands than between any other body part.

Throughout history, the open palm has been associated with truth, honesty, allegiance, and submission. Hidden palms may give a person an intuitive feeling that the person they are communicating with is untruthful. There many universal hand signals.

Objective—Demonstrate how to correctly use your hands in the open, authoritative, stop, caution, and directive.

Performance—Open, Authority, Stop, Caution, and Directive

1. Assume the bladed stance.
2. Position your arms with your elbows down and your palms facing upward = Open.
3. Position your arms with your elbows down and your palms down = Authority.
4. Position your arms extended and your palms facing outward = Stop.
5. Position your arms with your elbows down and your palms facing outward = Caution.
6. Position your arms/hands, pointing with your hand in the direction you want them to go = Directive.

Caution: Closing your hands into a fist position may send a message of aggression.

Caution: Do not point when giving, as pointing is perceived as a derogatory gesture.

Module 3: Contact and Cover Positioning

Contact and Cover (Team Positioning) is the main strategy for the Defensive Tactics System. Contact and Cover techniques are used by individuals during situations where they are dealing with a subject(s). The purpose of the technique is to deter a situation from getting out of control, and to improve the individual's safety by having other individuals in a constant state of preparation to act in the event that the situation gets out of control.

Contact (Team Leader)
The contact individual is the focal point for the subject as this individual is the primary communicator giving directions to the subject. In many situations, the contact individual(s) will initiate communications.

In the following information, the contact individual will be communicating with the subject, which may act as a distraction, allowing cover individuals (team members) to move in and gain physical control if needed. The contact individual should have a prearranged "cue" (verbal or non-verbal) alerting the cover individuals to initiate physical control.

Cover (Team Members)
The cover individual(s) role is to watch the subject(s) for any attempt to flee or assault the contact individual. The cover individual(s) should be ever vigilant and ready to respond and alert the contact individual of suspicious activity or an imminent attempt to assault the contact individual.

Special Note: Cover individuals should maintain their distance (stay back) until needed. Moving in too soon may cause the subject to feel as though he/she is being cornered.

Contact and Cover should be used for all situations involving subjects and witnesses.

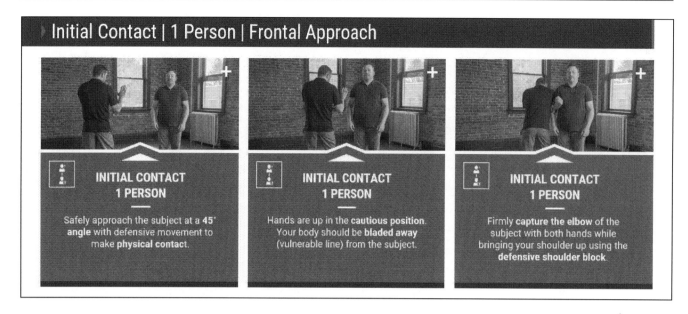

Initial Contact | 1 Person | Frontal Approach

INITIAL CONTACT 1 PERSON — Safely approach the subject at a **45° angle** with defensive movement to make **physical contact**.

INITIAL CONTACT 1 PERSON — Hands are up in the **cautious position**. Your body should be **bladed away** (vulnerable line) from the subject.

INITIAL CONTACT 1 PERSON — Firmly **capture the elbow** of the subject with both hands while bringing your shoulder up using the **defensive shoulder block**.

Initial Contact (1 person)

It is a technique that teaches individuals how to safely approach a subject and make initial contact.

Objective—Demonstrate how to safely approach a subject while moving forward with defensive movement to make physical contact.

Note: A two-person Initial Contact is safer as you have controlled both arms of the aggressor. This technique can be done to the front or behind the subject. It is safer to perform from behind the subject.

Performance—Initial Contact (1 person)

1. Move forward towards the subject at a 45-degree angle.

2. Use defensive movement and keep your hands in the caution position.

3. Your body should be bladed away (vulnerable line) from the subject. Left side forward on the left side of the subject, and right side forward on the right side of the subject.

4. Firmly capture the elbow of the subject with both hands (thumbs up).

5. Bring your shoulder slightly forward to further protect your vulnerable line if you are in front of the subject. Avoid this if you are behind the subject.

Caution: Armed individuals should keep the gun side back and away from the subject regardless of their approaching side.

Caution: Approaching a subject to the front is more dangerous for the individual than approaching from behind.

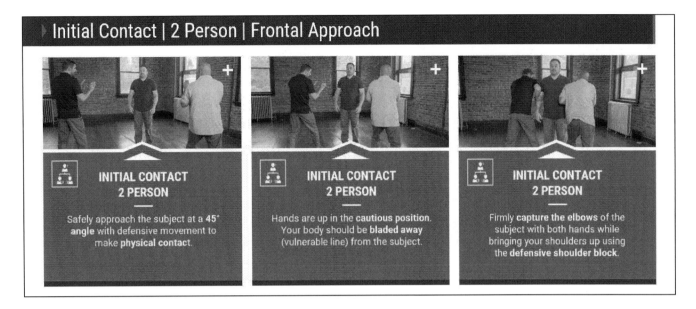

Initial Contact (2 person)

It is a technique that teaches individuals how to safely approach a subject and make contact.

Objective—Demonstrate how to safely approach a subject while moving forward with defensive movement to make physical contact.

Note: A two-person Initial Contact is safer as you have controlled both arms of the aggressor. This technique can be done to the front or behind the subject. It is safer to perform from behind the subject.

Performance—Initial Contact (2 person)

1. Move forward towards the subject at a 45-degree angle.

2. Use defensive movement and keep your hands in the caution position.

3. Your body should be bladed away (vulnerable line) from the subject. Left side forward on left of subject and right side forward on the right side of the subject.

4. Firmly capture the elbow of the subject with both hands (thumbs up).

5. Bring your shoulder slightly forward to further protect your vulnerable line if you are in front of the subject. Avoid this if you are behind the subject.

Caution: Armed individuals should keep the gun side back and away from the subject regardless of their approaching side.

Caution: Approaching a subject to the front is more dangerous for individuals than approaching from behind.

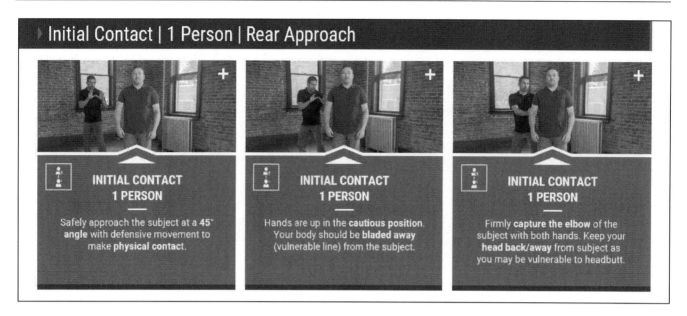

Initial Contact (1 person)

It is a technique that teaches individuals how to safely approach a subject and make initial contact.

Objective—Demonstrate how to safely approach a subject while moving forward with defensive movement to make physical contact.

Note: A two-person Initial Contact is safer as you have controlled both arms of the aggressor. This technique can be done to the front or behind the subject. It is safer to perform from behind the subject.

Performance—Initial Contact (1 person)

1. Move forward towards the subject at a 45-degree angle.
2. Use defensive movement and keep your hands in the caution position.
3. Your body can be (but not necessary) bladed away (vulnerable line) from the subject. Left side forward on left of subject and right side forward on the right side of the subject.
4. Firmly capture the elbow of the subject with both hands (thumbs up).

Caution: Armed individuals should keep the gun side back and away from the subject regardless of their approaching side.

Caution: Approaching a subject to the front is more dangerous for the individual than approaching from behind.

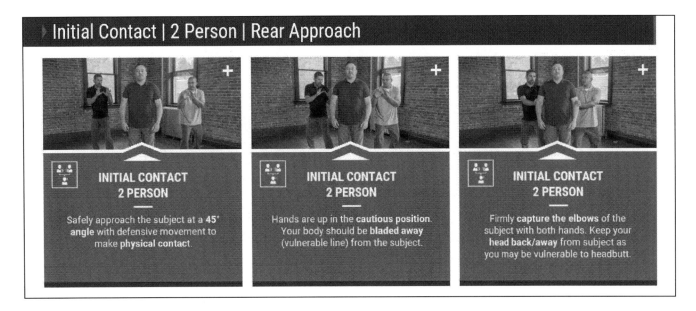

Initial Contact | 2 Person | Rear Approach

INITIAL CONTACT 2 PERSON — Safely approach the subject at a **45° angle** with defensive movement to make **physical contact**.

INITIAL CONTACT 2 PERSON — Hands are up in the **cautious position**. Your body should be **bladed away** (vulnerable line) from the subject.

INITIAL CONTACT 2 PERSON — Firmly **capture the elbows** of the subject with both hands. Keep your **head back/away** from subject as you may be vulnerable to headbutt.

Initial Contact (2 person)

It is a technique that teaches individuals how to safely approach a subject and make contact.

Objective—Demonstrate how to safely approach a subject while moving forward with defensive movement to make physical contact.

Note: A two-person Initial Contact is safer as you have controlled both arms of the aggressor This technique can be done to the front or behind the subject. It is safer to perform from behind the subject.

Performance—Initial Contact (1 or 2 person)

1. Move forward towards the subject at a 45-degree angle.
2. Use defensive movement and keep your hands in the caution position.
3. Your body can be (but not necessary) bladed away (vulnerable line) from the subject. Left side forward on left of subject and right side forward on the right side of the subject.
4. Firmly capture the elbow of the subject with both hands (thumbs up).

Caution: Armed individuals should keep the gun side back and away from the subject regardless of their approaching side.

Caution: Approaching a subject to the front is more dangerous for individuals than approaching from behind.

Contact and Cover (Team Positioning) is the main strategy for the AVADE® Defensive Tactics System. Contact and Cover techniques are used by individuals during situations where they are dealing with a subject(s). The purpose of the technique is to deter a situation from getting out of control, and to improve the individual's safety by having other individuals in a constant state of preparation to act in the event that the situation gets out of control.

Contact (Team Leader)

The contact individual is the focal point for the subject as this individual is the primary communicator giving directions to the subject. In many situations, the contact individual(s) will initiate communications.

In the pictures, the contact individual is communicating with the subject, which may act as a distraction, allowing cover individuals (team members) to move in and gain physical control if needed. The contact individual should have a prearranged "cue" (verbal or non-verbal) alerting the cover individuals to initiate physical control.

Cover (Team Members)

The cover individual(s) role is to watch the subject(s) for any attempt to flee or assault the contact individual. The cover individual(s) should be ever vigilant and ready to respond and alert the contact individual of suspicious activity or an imminent attempt to assault the contact individual.

Special Note: Cover individuals should maintain their distance (stay back) until needed (see top left picture). Moving in too soon may cause the subject to feel as though he/she is being cornered.

Contact and Cover should be used for all situations involving subjects and witnesses.

Module 4: Escort Strategies and Techniques

Escort (es-kawrt)
Definition of Escort
Noun
1. A group of persons, or a single person, accompanying another or others for protection, guidance, or courtesy.
2. An armed guard, as a body of soldiers or ships.
3. Protection, safeguard, or guidance on a journey.

   Verb (used with object)
1. To attend or accompany as an escort.

Strategy (strat-i-jee)
Definition of Strategy
Noun
1. Also strategics. the science or art of combining and employing the means of war in planning and directing large military movements and operations.
2. The use or an instance of using this science or art.
3. A plan, method, or series of maneuvers or stratagems for obtaining a specific goal or result.

Technique (tek-neek)
Definition of Technique
Noun
1. The manner and ability with which an artist, writer, dancer, athlete, or the like employs the technical skills of a particular art or field of endeavor.

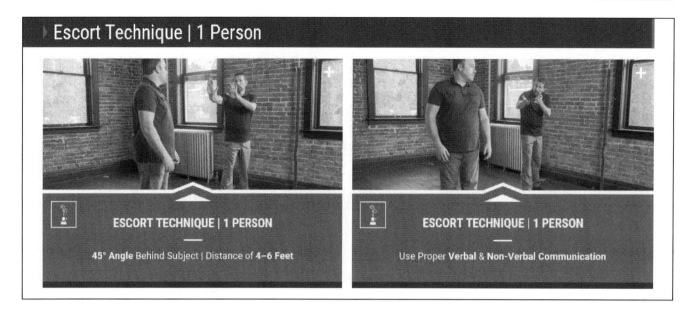

Escort Technique (1 person)

It is a technique that teaches individuals how to safely escort a cooperative subject.

Objective—Demonstrate how to safely escort a cooperative subject using proper distancing, verbal communications, and non-verbal communication.

Performance—Escort Technique (1 person)

1. Maintain a 45-degree angle and distance of (4-6 feet) behind the individual.

2. Direct subject to where you want them to go.

3. Use proper verbal and non-verbal skills.

4. Do not point; use open hand gestures.

5. Maintain Awareness.

Caution: If the subject stops and moves towards you, use verbal and non-verbal communication, and defensive movements.

The A-B-C's of the Escort Technique

A. Maintain a 45-degree angle & proper distance.

B. Direct individual where you want them to go.

C. Use your verbal and non-verbal skills.

D. Do not point with a finger (use hand)

E. Maintain awareness.

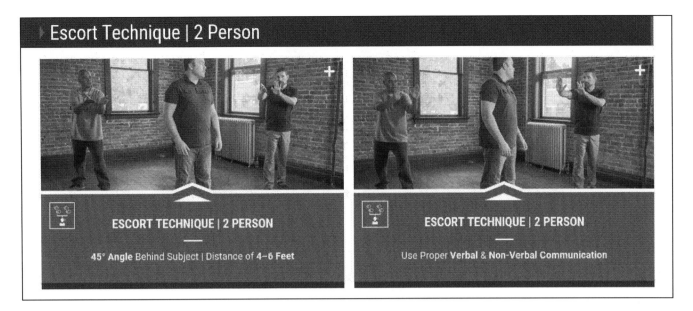

Escort Technique (2 person)

It is a technique that teaches individuals how to safely escort a cooperative subject.

Objective—Demonstrate how to safely escort a cooperative subject using proper distancing, verbal communications, and non-verbal communication.

Performance—Escort Technique (2 person)

1. Maintain a 45-degree angle and distance of 4-6 feet behind the individual.
2. Direct the subject where you want them to go.
3. Use proper verbal and non-verbal skills.
4. Do not point; use open hand gestures.
5. Maintain Awareness.

Caution: If the subject stops and moves towards you, use verbal and non-verbal communication and defensive movements.

The A-B-C's of the Escort Technique

A. Maintain a 45-degree angle & proper distance.
B. Direct individual where you want them to go.
C. Use your verbal and non-verbal skills.
D. Do not point with a finger (use hand)
E. Maintain awareness.

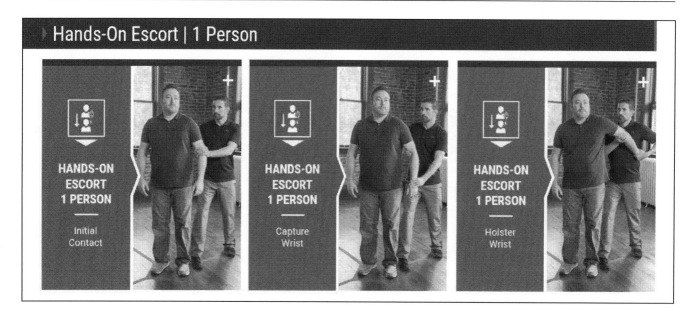

Hands-On Escort Technique (1 person)

It is a technique that teaches an individual how to escort a subject using light subject control.

Objective—Demonstrate how to safely escort a passive-resistive subject using light subject control with proper hand and body positioning.

Performance—Hands-On Escort (1 person)

1. From the initial contact position.
2. If you are on the right side of the subject, your right-hand slides down and grips the wrist. Same for the left side.
3. Bring the subject's gripped wrist to the side of your body (holstered position).
4. The subject's palm should be facing upward, and above any defensive tools, you may be carrying.
5. Maintain a 45-degree angle behind the subject and escort them to the desired location.

Caution: When gripping the appropriate wrist, the web of your hand should be on the ulna side of the subject's wrist. This ensures that their core strength is eliminated due to proper positioning.

Caution: When initiating the hands-on escort and when moving the subject, remember to stay at a 45-degree angle behind the subject.

Hands-On Escort | 2 Person

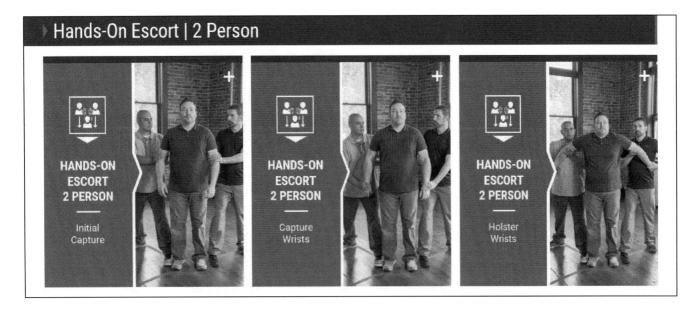

Hands-On Escort Technique (2 person)

It is a technique that teaches individuals how to escort a subject using light subject control.

Objective—Demonstrate how to safely escort a passive-resistive subject using light subject control with proper hand and body positioning.

Performance—Hands-On Escort (2 person)

1. From the initial contact position.
2. The individual on the right side of the subject will slide their right hand down and grip the wrist. Same for the left side.
3. Bring the subject's gripped wrist to the side of your body (holstered position).
4. The subject's palm should be facing upward, and above any defensive tools, you may be carrying.
5. Maintain a 45-degree angle behind the subject and escort them to the desired location.

Caution: When gripping the appropriate wrist, the web of your hand should be on the ulna side of the subject's wrist. This ensures that their core strength is eliminated due to proper positioning.

Caution: When initiating the hands-on escort and when moving the subject, remember to stay at a 45-degree angle behind the subject.

Caution: Both individuals acting with the same timing and control can reduce the possibility of escalation.

Module 5: Control and Decentralization Techniques

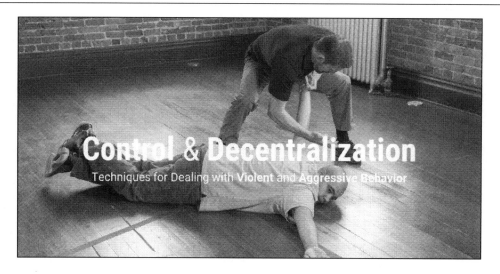

Control (Kuhn-trohl))
Definition of Control

Noun

1. The act or power of controlling; regulation; domination or command.

2. The situation of being under the regulation, domination, or command of another. Verb (used with object)

3. To exercise restraint or direction over; dominate: command.

4. To hold in check; curb:

Decentralize (dee-sen-truh-lahyz))
Definition of Decentralize

Verb

1. To distribute the administrative powers or functions of (a central authority) over a less concentrated area.

2. To disperse (something) from an area of concentration.

3. To undergo decentralization.

One Arm Take-Down (part 1)

It is a technique that teaches an individual how to decentralize a resistive subject using a take-down control technique.

Objective—Demonstrate how to control a subject using a one-bar take-down for a subject who is actively resisting.

Performance—One Arm Take-Down (part 1)

1. From the hands-on escort position.
2. The individual will place their wrist onto the tricep of the subject (2 -3" above the elbow).
3. The individual will then apply pressure to the tricep while moving forward or pivoting to the rear.
4. Use loud defensive verbalizations (NO, STOP, STOP RESISTING, WERE GOING DOWN, BREAK YOUR FALL, to direct the aggressor to stop resisting you and to direct them down.

Caution: Be aware of your environment and what direction you are moving the resistive subject towards.

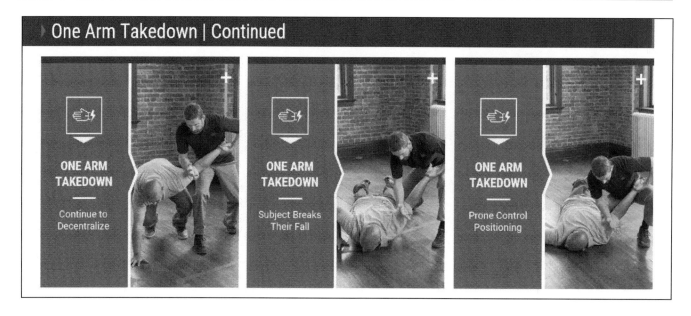

One-Arm Take-Down (part 2)

It is a technique that teaches an individual how to decentralize a resistive subject using a take-down control technique.

Objective—Demonstrate how to control a subject using a one-arm take-down for a subject who is actively resisting.

Performance—Arm-Bar Take-Down (part 2)

5. Continue to use movement and pressure on the tricep to direct the aggressor to the ground.

6. Use loud defensive verbalizations (NO, STOP, STOP RESISTING, WERE GOING DOWN, BREAK YOUR FALL, to direct the aggressor to stop resisting you and direct them down.

Caution: Be aware of your environment and what direction you are moving the resistive subject towards.

Caution: The prone position is a temporary position that may predispose the subject to breathing difficulties.

CONTINUOUSLY MONITOR THE SUBJECT & SEEK MEDICAL ATTENTION IF NEEDED.

Prone Control Position

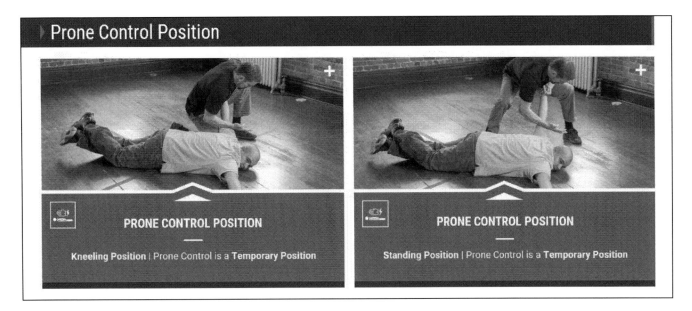

PRONE CONTROL POSITION

Kneeling Position | Prone Control is a **Temporary Position**

PRONE CONTROL POSITION

Standing Position | Prone Control is a **Temporary Position**

Prone Control Position CAUTION

- Individuals in a prone position may have difficulty breathing.

- Monitor individuals and place them on their side, seated position, or get them up as soon as possible.

PRONE CONTROL IS A TEMPORARY POSITION!

Positional asphyxia: Positional asphyxia is a form of asphyxia that occurs when someone's position prevents them from breathing adequately. A small but significant number of people die suddenly and without apparent reason during restraint by police, prison (corrections) officers, and health care staff. Positional asphyxia may be a factor in some of these deaths. Research has suggested that restraining a person in a face-down position is likely to cause greater restriction of breathing than restraining a person face-up. Many law enforcement and health personnel are now taught to avoid restraining people face down or to do so only for a very short period of time.

Prone Control Position | CAUTION

The **Prone Control Position** is a temporary position!

Individuals in a **prone position** may have **difficulty breathing**. Monitor the individuals and **place them** on their **side, seated** position, or **get them up** as soon as possible.

Standing the Prone Subject

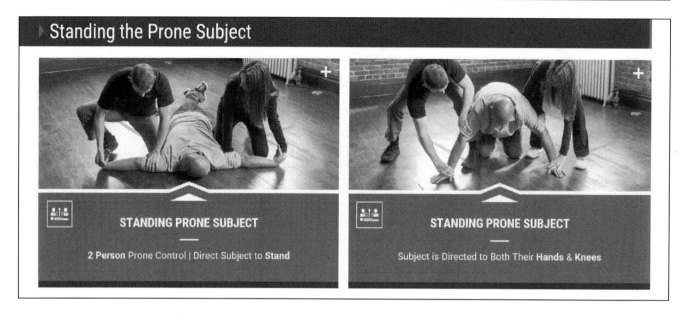

STANDING PRONE SUBJECT
—
2 Person Prone Control | Direct Subject to Stand

STANDING PRONE SUBJECT
—
Subject is Directed to Both Their Hands & Knees

Standing the Prone Subject (part 1)

It is a technique that teaches an individual(s) how to stand a prone controlled subject.

Objective—Demonstrate how to stand a subject that has been placed in a prone controlled position (one or two individuals are needed).

Performance—Standing the Prone Subject

1. Once control is established, verbalize to the subject to place their hands in the pushup position.

2. Direct them to push their knees up under them to prepare to stand.

3. Maintain contact with the subject arms and wrists and also prepare to stand up as well.

Caution: Verbalization and constant control is the key to standing a prone controlled subject. Maintain your balance and be prepared to escape if needed.

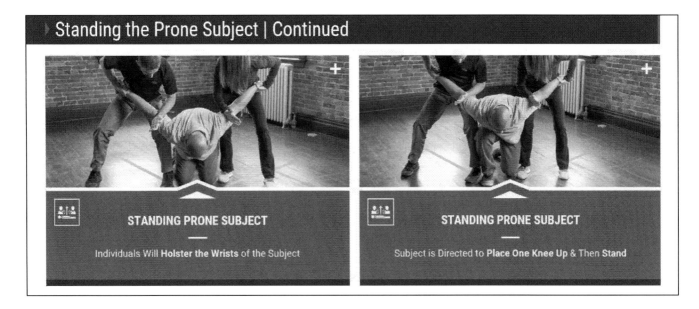

Standing the Prone Subject (part 2)

It is a technique that teaches an individual(s) how to stand a prone controlled subject.

Objective—Demonstrate how to stand a subject that has been placed in a prone controlled position (one or two individuals are needed).

Performance—Standing the Prone Subject

4. Bring one of the subject's wrists to the holster position on the side of your body.

5. Once control is established by holstering one wrist, the second person will holster the subject's other wrist.

6. Once both wrists are holstered, have the subject raise one knee.

7. You will need to have the subject raise their torso in order to get them to place one knee in front of them.

8. Ask the subject to then stand up completely. Direct the subject where you want them to go.

Caution: Verbalization and constant control is the key to standing a prone controlled subject. Maintain your balance and be prepared to escape if needed.

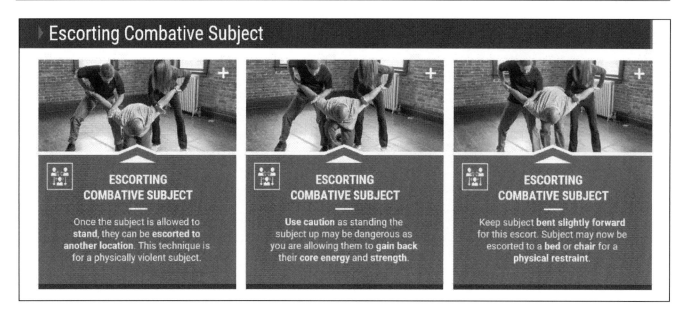

Escorting Combative Subject Technique

It is a technique that teaches an individual(s) how to escort a combative/violent subject.

Objective—Demonstrate how to escort a combative/violent subject using the combative subject escort technique (one or two individuals are needed).

Performance—Escorting Combative Subject Technique

1. From the kneeling position have the subject raise one knee.
2. You will need to have the subject raise their torso in order to get them to place one knee in front of them.
3. Ask the subject to then bring their other knee up and stand in a bent over position.
4. From this position (combative escort), you can direct the subject to another location for a wall control technique, or to a bed for a supine restraint.
5. Use loud, repetitive defensive verbalizations (NO, STOP, STOP RESISTING, to direct the aggressor to stop resisting you.

Caution: Verbalization and constant control is the key to controlling a combative subject. Maintain your balance and be prepared to escape if needed.

▸ Rear Arm Control

Rear Arm Control Technique (part 1)

It is a technique that teaches an individual how to control a resistive subject from the escort technique.

Objective—Demonstrate how to control a resistive subject using the rear arm control technique from the hands-on escort position (one or two individuals are needed).

Performance—Rear Arm Control Technique (part 1)

1. From the hands-on escort position.
2. The subject becomes resistive by pushing their arm backward.
3. The individual moves with the resistance and repositions him/herself turning 90 degrees towards the aggressor.
4. The individual pulls the resistive subjects' arm into his/her core.
5. Use loud, repetitive defensive verbalizations (NO, STOP, STOP RESISTING, to direct the aggressor to stop resisting you.

Caution: Tuck your head into the shoulder of the aggressor. This will prevent the aggressor from striking you with a rear head butt.

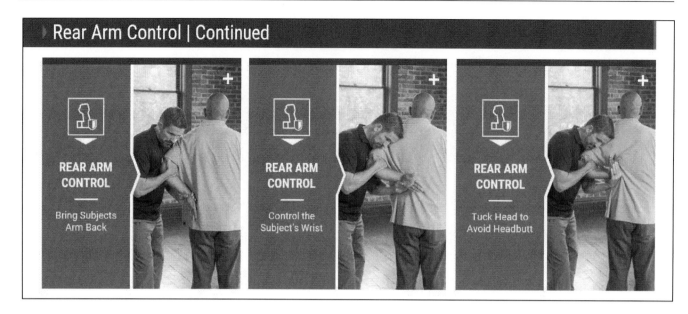

Rear Arm Control Technique (part 2)

It is a technique that teaches an individual how to control a resistive subject from the escort technique.

Objective—Demonstrate how to control a resistive subject using the rear arm control technique from the hands-on escort position (one or two individuals are needed).

Performance—Rear Arm Control Technique (part 2)

6. Continue to control the arm in your core by pulling it into you.
7. Reposition your hand on the wrist; bring your fingertips onto the resistive subject's knuckles.
8. Gently bring the subject's arm upward into their lower back as you bring the subject's fingertips towards you.
9. Use loud, repetitive defensive verbalizations (NO, STOP, STOP RESISTING, to direct the aggressor to stop resisting you.

From the rear arm control, you can:
- Escort the subject and/or handcuff the subject!

Caution: Tuck your head into the shoulder of the resistive subject. This will prevent the subject from striking you with a rear head butt.

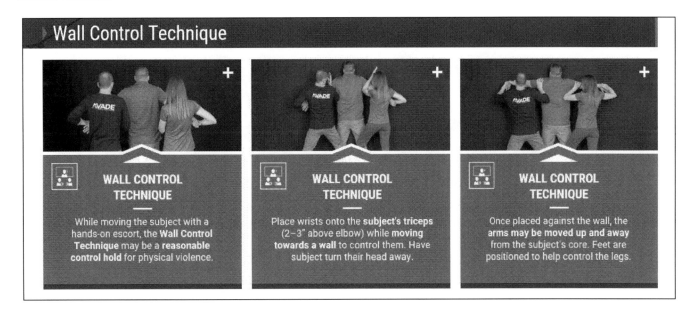

Wall Control Technique

It is a technique that teaches an individual how to decentralize and control a resistive subject and place them against a wall. This technique is for a subject who displays violent or self- destructive behavior towards themselves or others.

Objective—Demonstrate how to control a resistive subject using the wall control technique from the hands-on escort position (two individuals are needed).

Performance—Wall Control Technique

1. From the hands-on escort position.
2. The individuals will place their wrist onto the tricep of the subject (2 -3" above the elbow) while walking the subject towards a wall.
3. Continue to place the individual on the wall (have subject turn their head to the side) and position your feet closest to the subject on the inside of their feet.
4. Bring the subject's arms out to the side and continue to use your wrist or hands on the subject's triceps.
5. Use loud, repetitive defensive verbalizations (NO, STOP, STOP RESISTING, to direct the aggressor to stop resisting you.

Caution: Be aware of your environment and what direction you are moving the resistive subject towards.

Caution: The wall control position is a temporary position that may predispose the subject to breathing difficulties.

CONTINUOUSLY MONITOR THE SUBJECT AND SEEK MEDICAL ATTENTION IF NEEDED.

Module 6: Handcuffing Techniques

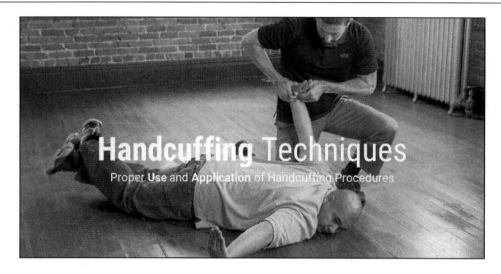

Personal Safety Training Inc. (PSTI) does not endorse any specific handcuff manufacture. PSTI does however, recommend that agencies use a recognized public safety grade handcuff that is NIJ (national institute of justice) approved. https://www.ojp.gov/pdffiles1/nij/082981.pdf

Chain Handcuffs: Chain handcuffs are the most commonly used handcuffs. These handcuffs have a short chain between the cuffs and are relatively flexible because of the chain. The additional mobility and flexibility of the swivels on the cuffs make them ideal for getting the cuffs on subjects.

Hinged Handcuffs: Hinged handcuffs have a hinge that bends in the middle. These handcuffs are more rigid and restraining in design because the wrists of the suspect are held closer together, and movement is more limited. Hinged handcuffs may be smaller than traditional handcuffs and may be challenging to use for officers with larger hands.

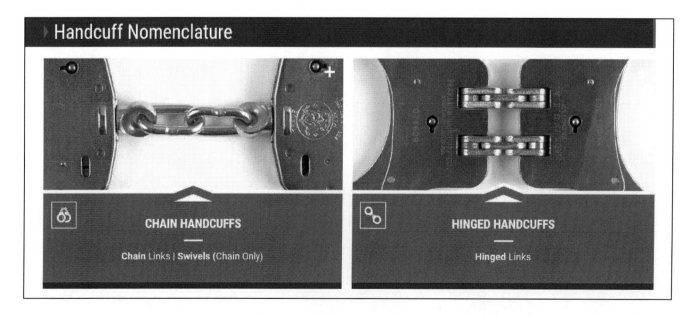

▶ Handcuff Nomenclature | Continued

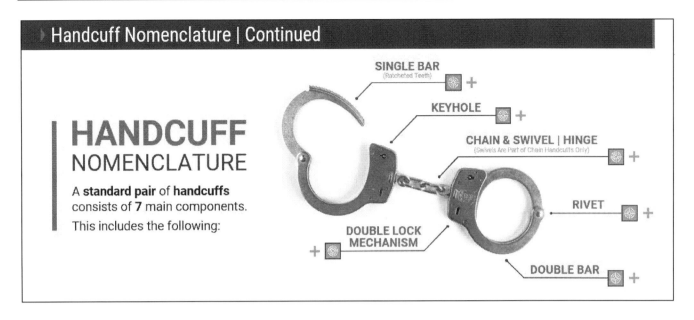

HANDCUFF
NOMENCLATURE

A **standard pair** of **handcuffs** consists of **7** main components. This includes the following:

SINGLE BAR
(Ratcheted Teeth)

KEYHOLE

CHAIN & SWIVEL | HINGE
(Swivels Are Part of Chain Handcuffs Only)

RIVET

DOUBLE BAR

DOUBLE LOCK MECHANISM

▶ Loading Your Handcuffs

HANDCUFF
QUICKLY & SMOOTHLY

Always carry your **handcuffs** in the **"loaded"** position. This will allow the officer to apply them more **quickly** and **smoothly** to a subject's wrist.

MARKER
(Loaded Handcuffs)

MARKER
(Loaded Handcuffs)

Loading Your Handcuffs

Always carry your handcuffs in the "loaded" position by pushing the single bar through the ratchet in the body of the cuff until it is almost through (2-4 teeth remain in contact with the ratchet). The tip of the single bar may extend through and beyond the body of the cuff. Loaded handcuffs allow the officer to apply them more quickly and smoothly to a subject's wrist.

Care & Maintenance of Handcuffs

- Follow Manufacturer Guidelines.
- Make sure single bars on handcuffs will cycle through easily.
- Avoid contact with moisture.
- Disinfect if exposed to body fluids.
- Use an oil (light oil) at swivel, rivet, and hinge areas only, and wipe excess oil away.

Handcuffing Stance & Grip | Chain Handcuffs

HANDCUFFING STANCE

Chain Handcuffs are held in a **pistol grip position** allowing the **single bars** to **rotate** through completely.

HANDCUFFING GRIP POSITION

Chain Handcuffs are held in a **pistol grip position** allowing the **single bars** to **rotate** through completely.

Handcuffing Stance & Grip | Hinged Handcuffs

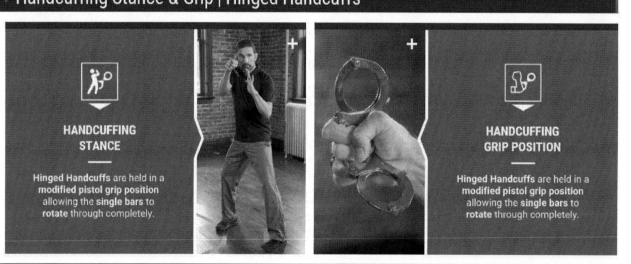

HANDCUFFING STANCE

Hinged Handcuffs are held in a **modified pistol grip position** allowing the **single bars** to **rotate** through completely.

HANDCUFFING GRIP POSITION

Hinged Handcuffs are held in a **modified pistol grip position** allowing the **single bars** to **rotate** through completely.

Handcuff Key | Handcuff Holder

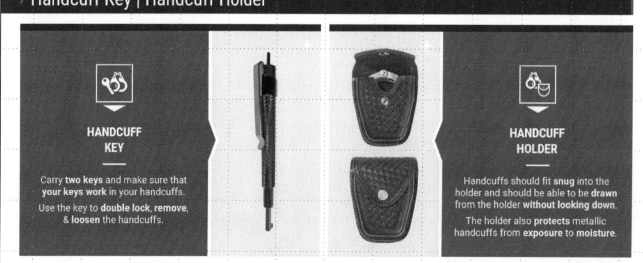

HANDCUFF KEY

Carry **two keys** and make sure that **your keys work** in your handcuffs.

Use the key to **double lock**, **remove**, & **loosen** the handcuffs.

HANDCUFF HOLDER

Handcuffs should fit **snug** into the holder and should be able to be **drawn** from the holder **without looking down**.

The holder also **protects** metallic handcuffs from **exposure** to **moisture**.

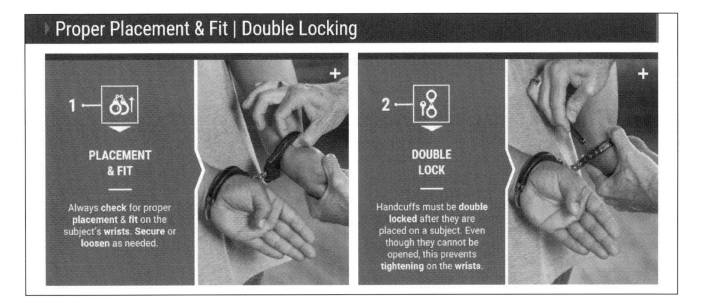

Proper Placement & Fit | Double Locking

1 — PLACEMENT & FIT
Always **check** for proper **placement & fit** on the subject's **wrists**. **Secure** or **loosen** as needed.

2 — DOUBLE LOCK
Handcuffs must be **double locked** after they are placed on a subject. Even though they cannot be opened, this prevents **tightening** on the **wrists**.

Check for Proper Fit and Wrist Placement

Handcuffs should be placed correctly at the smallest part of the wrist, just above the palm. Once positioned correctly, the officer should be able to touch his/her tip of their index finger and thumb together. Important to check proper fit in more than one area of the subject's wrist.

- When placed above the wrists, injuries can occur.

- Handcuffs should NOT be placed to secure (tight) or too loose on the subject's wrist.

- Always check for proper fit and placement on the wrists. Secure or loosen as needed.

Always Double Lock Handcuffs

Handcuffs should be double locked for the safety of the subject, the officer, and the public. The pin end of the handcuff key is placed into the double locking mechanism to secure the handcuff from tightening. Note: The double locking mechanism is not in the same place on all handcuffs. Officers should be aware of their handcuff nomenclature (parts and pieces).

It is very important that handcuffs are double locked after they are placed on a subject. Even though the handcuffs cannot be opened, if they are not double-locked, they can become more secure (tightened) on the wrists. It is the tightening effect that can cause damage and injury to the subject. This can lead to lawsuits against agencies and officers.

PROPER PLACEMENT – PROPER FIT – DOUBLE LOCK

Standing Handcuffing

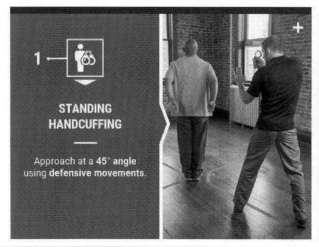

1

STANDING HANDCUFFING

Approach at a **45°** angle using **defensive movements**.

2

STANDING HANDCUFFING

With your **control hand, grip** the subject's **hand** using a **reverse handshake position** (Thumb-to-Thumb).

Standing Handcuffing | Continued

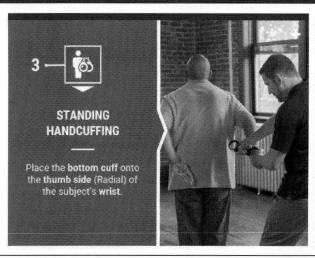

3

STANDING HANDCUFFING

Place the **bottom cuff** onto the **thumb side** (Radial) of the subject's **wrist**.

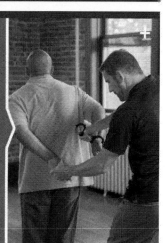

4

STANDING HANDCUFFING

Release your **control hand** & grip the subject's **free hand** using a **handshake position** (Thumb-to-Thumb).

Standing Handcuffing | Continued

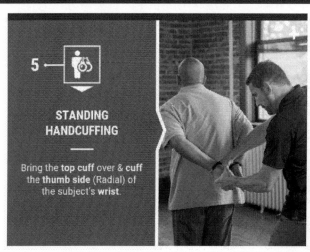

5

STANDING HANDCUFFING

Bring the **top cuff** over & **cuff** the **thumb side** (Radial) of the subject's **wrist**.

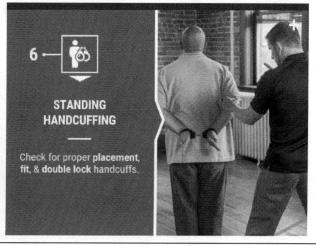

6

STANDING HANDCUFFING

Check for proper **placement, fit**, & **double lock** handcuffs.

Standing Handcuffing Technique

It is a technique that teaches officers how to handcuff a subject who is cooperative or semi-cooperative in a standing position.

Objective—Demonstrate how to position, approach, and safely handcuff a cooperative or semi-cooperative subject who is in a standing position.

Performance—Standing Handcuffing Technique (part 1)

1. Before entering into the reactionary gap, position the subject facing away from you and looking upward.

2. The subject should have their hands behind them away from their body.

3. The feet of the subject can be together or separated. Follow agency guidelines.

4. Approach at a 45-degree angle using defensive movement.

5. With your control hand, grip the subject's hand using a reverse handshake (thumb-to-thumb).

6. Place the bottom cuff onto the thumb side (radial) of the subject's wrist.

7. After the first cuff is applied, release your control hand and grip the subject's free hand using a handshake position (thumb-to-thumb).

8. Bring the top cuff over and cuff the thumb side (radial) of the wrist.

9. Check for proper placement and proper fit on both handcuffed wrists. Adjust if needed.

10. Double lock handcuffs.

Caution: Most resistance occurs after the first cuff has been applied. Maintain awareness and be prepared to escape or utilize a decentralizing technique if needed.

FOLLOW AGENCY POLICY AND PROCEDURE FOR SEARCHING THE SUBJECT.

Kneeling Handcuffing

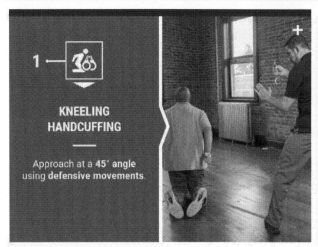

1

KNEELING HANDCUFFING

Approach at a **45°** angle using **defensive movements**.

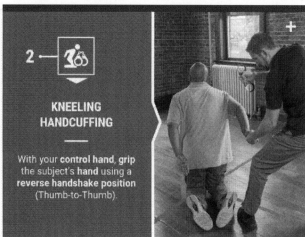

2

KNEELING HANDCUFFING

With your **control hand**, grip the subject's **hand** using a **reverse handshake position** (Thumb-to-Thumb).

Kneeling Handcuffing | Continued

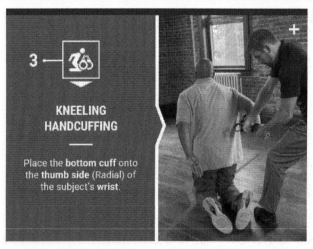

3

KNEELING HANDCUFFING

Place the **bottom cuff** onto the **thumb side** (Radial) of the subject's **wrist**.

4

KNEELING HANDCUFFING

Release your **control hand** & grip the subject's **free hand** using a **handshake position** (Thumb-to-Thumb).

Kneeling Handcuffing | Continued

5

KNEELING HANDCUFFING

Bring the **top cuff** over & **cuff** the **thumb side** (Radial) of the subject's **wrist**.

6

KNEELING HANDCUFFING

Check for proper **placement, fit,** & **double lock** handcuffs.

Kneeling Handcuffing Technique

It is a technique that teaches officers how to handcuff a subject who is cooperative, semi-cooperative, or uncooperative in a kneeling position.

Objective—Demonstrate how to position, approach, and safely handcuff a cooperative, semi-cooperative, or uncooperative subject who is in a kneeling position.

Performance—Kneeling Handcuffing Technique (part 1)

1. Before entering into the reactionary gap, position the subject facing away from you and looking upward.

2. The subject should have their hands behind them away from their body.

3. The feet of the subject can be together or crossed. Follow agency guidelines.

4. Approach at a 45-degree angle using defensive movement.

5. With your control hand, grip the subject's hand using a reverse handshake (thumb-to-thumb).

6. Place the bottom cuff onto the thumb side (radial) of the subject's wrist.

7. After the first cuff is applied, release your control hand and grip the subject's free hand using a handshake position (thumb-to-thumb).

8. Bring the top cuff over and cuff the thumb side (radial) of the wrist.

9. Check for proper placement and proper fit on both handcuffed wrists. Adjust if needed.

10. Double lock handcuffs.

Caution: Most resistance occurs after the first cuff has been applied. Maintain awareness and be prepared to escape or utilize a decentralizing technique if needed.

FOLLOW AGENCY POLICY AND PROCEDURE FOR SEARCHING THE SUBJECT.

Prone Handcuffing

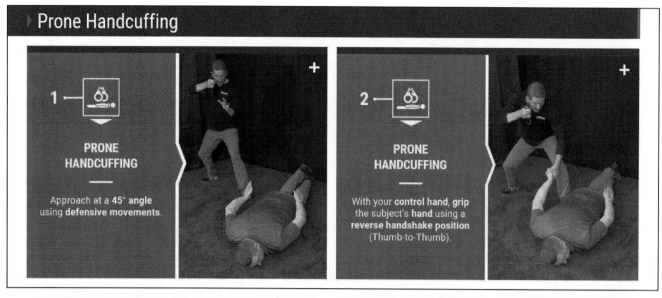

1 — PRONE HANDCUFFING

Approach at a **45° angle** using **defensive movements**.

2 — PRONE HANDCUFFING

With your **control hand, grip** the subject's **hand** using a **reverse handshake position** (Thumb-to-Thumb).

Prone Handcuffing | Continued

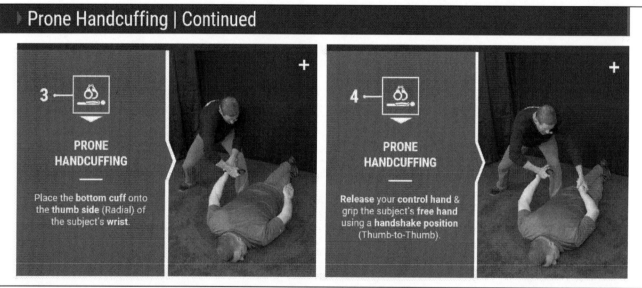

3 — PRONE HANDCUFFING

Place the **bottom cuff** onto the **thumb side** (Radial) of the subject's **wrist**.

4 — PRONE HANDCUFFING

Release your **control hand** & grip the subject's **free hand** using a **handshake position** (Thumb-to-Thumb).

Prone Handcuffing | Continued

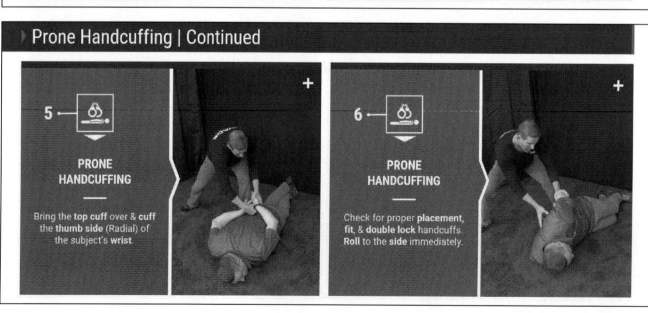

5 — PRONE HANDCUFFING

Bring the **top cuff** over & **cuff** the **thumb side** (Radial) of the subject's **wrist**.

6 — PRONE HANDCUFFING

Check for proper **placement, fit,** & **double lock** handcuffs. **Roll** to the **side** immediately.

Prone Handcuffing Technique

It is a technique that teaches officers how to handcuff a subject who is cooperative, semi-cooperative, or uncooperative in a prone position.

Objective—Demonstrate how to position, approach, and safely handcuff a cooperative, semi-cooperative, or uncooperative subject who is in a prone position.

Performance—Prone Handcuffing Technique

1. Before entering into the reactionary gap, position the subject face-down and looking away from you.

2. The subject should have their hands/arms up and behind their back with their palms up.

3. The feet of the subject can be together or crossed. Follow agency guidelines.

4. Approach at a 45-degree angle using defensive movement.

5. With your control hand, grip the subject's hand using a reverse handshake (thumb-to-thumb).

6. Place the bottom cuff onto the thumb side (radial) of the subject's wrist.

7. After the first cuff is applied, release your control hand and grip the subject's free hand using a handshake position (thumb-to-thumb).

8. Bring the top cuff over and cuff the (radial) thumb side of the wrist.

9. Check for proper placement and proper fit on both handcuffed wrists. Adjust if needed. Double lock handcuffs.

10. Roll the subject to their side and prepare to move the subject into a seated position or standing position. Prone control is a temporary position! See technique: Standing the Prone Handcuffed Subject

Caution: Do not place knee onto the head, neck, or spine of the subject
Caution: Individuals in a prone position may have difficulty breathing. Monitor individuals and place them on their side, seated position, them up as soon as possible.
Caution: Prone Control is a temporary position!
Caution: Most resistance occurs after the first cuff has been applied.

FOLLOW AGENCY POLICY AND PROCEDURE FOR SEARCHING THE SUBJECT.

▸ Prone Handcuffing | Partner Assisted

1 — **PARTNER ASSISTED HANDCUFFING**

From the **2-Person Hands-On Escort** technique.

2 — **PARTNER ASSISTED HANDCUFFING**

One Officer will **release** or **disengage** while the other officer takes the subject down with a **One Arm Takedown** technique.

▸ Prone Handcuffing | Partner Assisted | Continued

3 — **PARTNER ASSISTED HANDCUFFING**

Once the subject is **down**, the Officer will maintain the subject in a **Prone Control Position** while directing the subject to **raise their non-controlled arm** in the air.

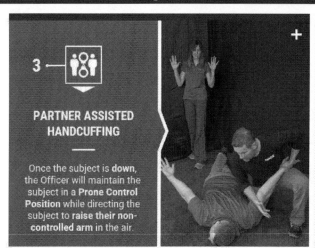

4 — **PARTNER ASSISTED HANDCUFFING**

The disengaged Officer will **move in** and with their **control hand**, grip the subject's **hand** using a **reverse handshake** (Thumb-to-Thumb) & **cuff** the subject's **wrist**.

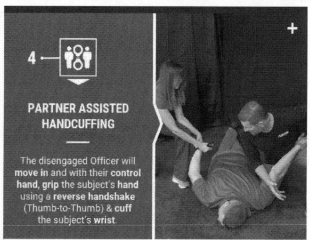

▸ Prone Handcuffing | Partner Assisted | Continued

5 — **PARTNER ASSISTED HANDCUFFING**

The controlling Officer will release subject's **arm** & bring it into the subject's **lower back**, allowing partner to handcuff the **secondary wrist** of the subject.

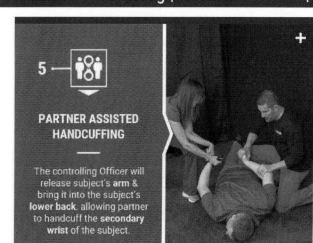

6 — **PARTNER ASSISTED HANDCUFFING**

Check for proper **placement**, **fit**, & **double lock** handcuffs. **Roll to the side** immediately.

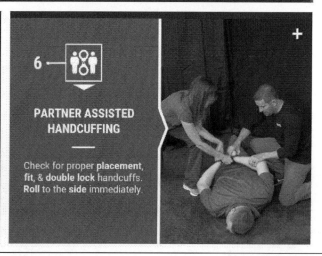

Prone Handcuffing Partner Assisted Technique

It is a technique that teaches officers how to decentralize and handcuff a subject who is uncooperative in a prone position.

Objective—Demonstrate how to position, decentralize, and safely take-down an uncooperative subject to the prone position and have your partner assist in handcuffing them.

Performance—Prone Handcuffing Partner Assisted Technique

1. From the two-person hands-on escort technique.

2. One officer will release/disengage while the other officer takes the subject down with the one arm take-down technique.

3. Use loud defensive verbalizations (NO, STOP, STOP RESISTING, WERE GOING DOWN, BREAK YOUR FALL, to direct the aggressor to stop resisting you and direct them down.

4. Once the subject is down, the officer will maintain a subject-prone control position while directing the subject to raise their non-controlled arm into the air.

5. The officer who disengaged will now move in, and with their control hand, grip the subject's hand using a reverse handshake (thumb-to-thumb).

6. The same officer will place the bottom cuff onto the thumb side (radial) of the subject's wrist.

7. Once the handcuff is placed correctly on the subject's wrist, the officer controlling the subject will safely release the controlled arm and bring it into the subjects lower back allowing the partner/officer to handcuff the secondary radial wrist of the subject.

8. Officers will check for proper placement and proper fit on both handcuffed wrists. Adjust if needed and double lock handcuffs.

9. An officer will roll the subject to their side and prepare to move the subject into a seated position or standing position. Prone control is a temporary position!
    See technique: Standing the Prone Handcuffed Subject

Caution: Be aware of your environment and what direction you are moving the resistive subject towards.
Caution: The prone position is a temporary position that may predispose the subject to breathing difficulties.

CONTINUOUSLY MONITOR THE SUBJECT & SEEK MEDICAL ATTENTION IF NEEDED.

▶ Prone Position | **CAUTION**

The **Prone Position** is a **temporary position!**

Individuals in a **prone position** may have **difficulty breathing. Monitor** the individuals and **place them** on their **side**, **seated** position, or **get them up** as soon as possible.

▶ Standing the Prone Handcuffed Subject

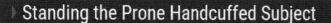

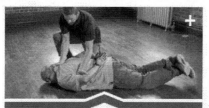

STANDING PRONE HANDCUFFED SUBJECT

Position yourself on the **side** of the subject with one **hand supporting** the **head & neck** & your other **hand gripping** the **inside** of the **elbow**.

STANDING PRONE HANDCUFFED SUBJECT

Using the **momentum** of the subject, **rock & assist** them **towards** you & into the **seated** position.

STANDING PRONE HANDCUFFED SUBJECT

If on the right **side** of the subject, place your right **arm** across their **shoulder**. Same on the left side. With your opposite **hand**, **grip** the **elbow**, preparing to **rock** the subject onto their **knees**.

▶ Standing the Prone Handcuffed Subject | Continued

STANDING PRONE HANDCUFFED SUBJECT

Using the **momentum** of the subject, **rock & assist** them onto their **knees**.

STANDING PRONE HANDCUFFED SUBJECT

Have the subject place a **foot** up **in front** of themselves.

STANDING PRONE HANDCUFFED SUBJECT

Using the **momentum** of the subject, **rock & assist** them onto their **feet**.

Standing the Prone Handcuffed Subject

It is a technique that teaches officers how to stand a prone handcuffed subject.

Objective—Demonstrate how to position and safely stand a handcuffed subject who is in a prone position.

Performance—Standing the Prone Handcuffed Subject

1. Position yourself on the side of the subject with one hand supporting the head and neck palm up) and your other hand gripping the inside of the elbow (palm up).

2. Using the momentum of the subject, rock them towards you, and assist them into a seated position.

3. Once the subject is seated, position yourself on either side of the subject.

4. If on the right side of the subject, place your right arm across their shoulder. Same for the left side.

5. With your opposite hand, grip their elbow, preparing to rock the subject onto their knees.

6. Using the momentum of the subject, rock them and assist them onto their knees.

7. With the subject in the kneeling position, maintain your hand position.

8. Have the subject bring their right foot up in from of them if you are on their right side. Same for left side.

9. Using the momentum of the subject, rock them and assist them onto their feet.

Caution: Avoid lifting the subject up using your back (muscles) as injuries to officers are highly probable.

Caution: Maintain control of the subject when rocking them onto their knees to avoid the subject falling forward.

Caution: Maintain awareness as the subject is now mobile and may be a higher risk to the officer in this position.

CONTINUOUSLY MONITOR THE SUBJECT & SEEK MEDICAL ATTENTION IF NEEDED.

Escorting Handcuffed Subjects

COOPERATIVE SUBJECTS

Maintain a **45° angle** behind the subject. Use your **hand** closest to the subject (Inside Elbow Joint) to **guide** the subject.

UNCOOPERATIVE SUBJECTS

Maintain a **45° angle** behind the subject. Use your **hand** closest to the subject to **control** their **hand**, use your other **hand** to **control** the subject's **elbow**.

Handcuffing Tips & Warnings

☑ Follow your **handcuffing policies** & **procedures**

☑ Never **underestimate** anyone!

☑ Subjects can **head butt**, **bite**, **knee**, **elbow**, & **spit** on you while in handcuffs

☑ Handcuffs are **mechanical tools** & may **malfunction**. Have an **Escape Plan**!

☑ Place handcuffs on as **quickly as possible**

Handcuffing Tips & Warnings | Continued

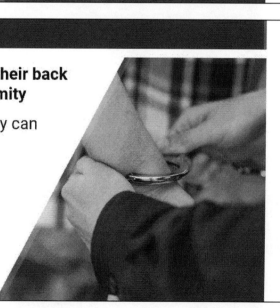

☑ Handcuff subjects with their **hands behind their back** unless they have an **injury** or obvious **deformity**

☑ Avoid placing subjects **against anything** they can **push off of** | Cars, Walls, etc.

☑ Always check for **proper placement**, **fit**, & **double lock** the handcuffs

☑ Always **repeat the above** every **15 minutes** if the subject is handcuffed

☑ Always **document** the above

Module 7: Defensive Blocking Techniques

During & After All Defenses

During all defenses use loud and repetitive defensive verbalizations (NO, STOP, GET BACK, STOP RESISTING, etc.) to direct the aggressor to stop attacking you, as well as using defensive movements - Escape!

After all defenses be sure to follow agency policies and procedures in regard to self-defense. Report and document immediately.

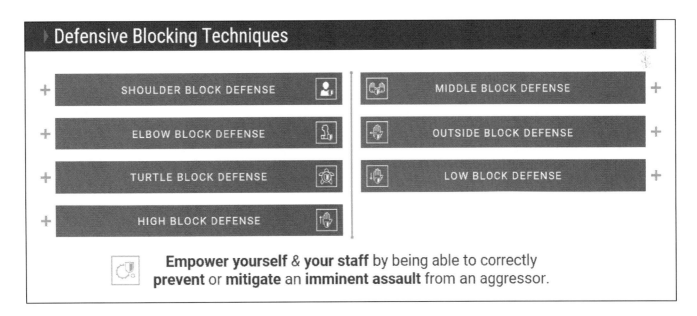

Defensive Blocking Techniques

SHOULDER BLOCK DEFENSE	MIDDLE BLOCK DEFENSE
ELBOW BLOCK DEFENSE	OUTSIDE BLOCK DEFENSE
TURTLE BLOCK DEFENSE	LOW BLOCK DEFENSE
HIGH BLOCK DEFENSE	

Empower yourself & your staff by being able to correctly **prevent** or **mitigate** an **imminent assault** from an aggressor.

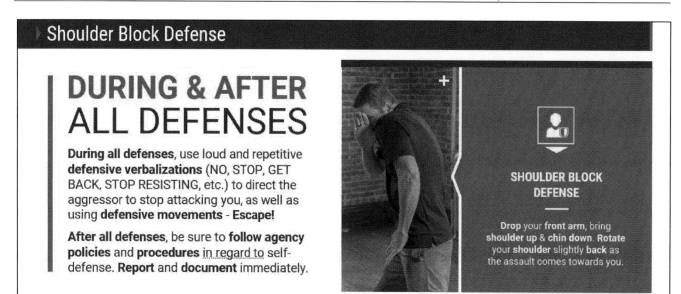

> **Shoulder Block Defense**

DURING & AFTER ALL DEFENSES

During all defenses, use loud and repetitive **defensive verbalizations** (NO, STOP, GET BACK, STOP RESISTING, etc.) to direct the aggressor to stop attacking you, as well as using **defensive movements - Escape!**

After all defenses, be sure to **follow agency policies** and **procedures** in regard to self-defense. **Report** and **document** immediately.

SHOULDER BLOCK DEFENSE

Drop your **front arm**, bring **shoulder up & chin down**. Rotate your **shoulder** slightly **back** as the assault comes towards you.

Shoulder Block Defense

It is a technique that teaches individuals how to deflect an imminent assault.

Objective—Demonstrate how to properly use a defensive shoulder block against a physical assault to your head.

Performance—Shoulder Block Defense

1. Assume the bladed stance.

2. Bring your chin down.

3. Drop the arm that is in front of you while bringing your shoulder up to your chin.

4. You can slightly rotate your body towards your backside as the assault comes towards you, further deflecting the attack.

During all Defenses:

▪ Use loud, repetitive defensive verbalizations (NO, STOP, GET BACK, STOP RESISTING, etc.) to direct the aggressor to stop attacking you.

▪ Use defensive movements (Escape!)

After all Defenses:

▪ Follow agency policies and procedures in regard to self-defense.

▪ Report and Document immediately.

> ▸ **Elbow Block Defense**

DURING & AFTER ALL DEFENSES

During all defenses, use loud and repetitive **defensive verbalizations** (NO, STOP, GET BACK, STOP RESISTING, etc.) to direct the aggressor to stop attacking you, as well as using **defensive movements - Escape!**

After all defenses, be sure to **follow agency policies** and **procedures** in regard to self-defense. **Report** and **document** immediately.

ELBOW BLOCK DEFENSE

Use your **front arm & elbow** to **create a shield** in front of your **face**.

Elbow Block Defense

It is a technique that teaches individuals how to deflect an imminent assault.

Objective—Demonstrate how to properly use a defensive elbow block against a physical assault to your head.

Performance—Elbow Block Defense

1. Assume the bladed stance.

2. Bring your chin down.

3. Bring your front arm up to your face with your elbow directly in front, creating a shield in front of your face.

4. You can slightly rotate your body towards your backside as the assault comes towards you, further deflecting the attack.

During all Defenses:

- Use loud, repetitive defensive verbalizations (NO, STOP, GET BACK, STOP RESISTING, etc.) to direct the aggressor to stop attacking you.

- Use defensive movements (Escape!)

After all Defenses:

- Follow agency policies and procedures in regard to self-defense.

- Report and Document immediately.

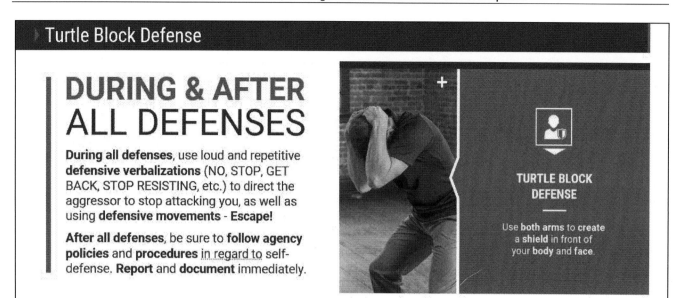

Turtle Block Defense

It is a technique that teaches individuals how to deflect an imminent assault.

Objective—Demonstrate how to properly use a defensive turtle block against a physical assault to your head and torso.

Performance—Turtle Block Defense

1. Assume the bladed stance.

2. Bring your chin down.

3. Bring both arms up in front of your face with your elbows directly in front, creating a shield in front of your and body face.

4. You can slightly rotate your body towards your backside as the assault comes towards you, further deflecting the attack.

During all Defenses:

- Use loud, repetitive defensive verbalizations (NO, STOP, GET BACK, STOP RESISTING, etc.) to direct the aggressor to stop attacking you.

- Use defensive movements (Escape!)

After all Defenses:

- Follow agency policies and procedures in regard to self-defense.

- Report and Document immediately.

⟩ High Block Defense

High Block Defense

It is a technique that teaches individuals how to deflect an imminent assault to their head.

Objective—Demonstrate how to properly use a high defensive block against a physical assault to your head.

Performance—High Block Defense

1. Assume the bladed stance.

2. Bring your chin down.

3. Bring your arm up in front of your face with your palm out.

4. Your hands can be open or closed.

5. You can use your support arm, strong arm, or both arms to defend against an attack on your head

During all Defenses:

- Use loud, repetitive defensive verbalizations (NO, STOP, GET BACK, STOP RESISTING, etc.) to direct the aggressor to stop attacking you.

- Use defensive movements (Escape!)

After all Defenses:

- Follow agency policies and procedures in regard to self-defense.

- Report and Document immediately.

Middle Block Defense

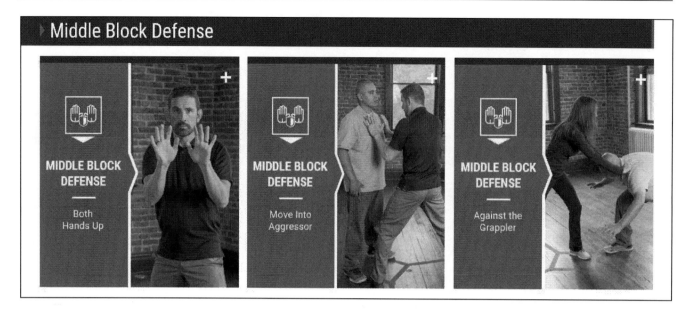

Middle Block Defense

It is a technique that teaches individuals how to deflect an imminent rushing assault or grappling attack towards you.

Objective—Demonstrate how to properly use a defensive middle block against a physical assault coming at you.

Performance—Middle Block Defense

1. Assume the bladed stance.
2. Bring both arms up in front of you (palms out).
3. Push the aggressor away at the shoulders or torso area.
4. Use side-to-side movement after the middle block defense to get into a position of advantage or to continue to defend.

During all Defenses:

- Use loud, repetitive defensive verbalizations (NO, STOP, GET BACK, STOP RESISTING, etc.) to direct the aggressor to stop attacking you.

- Use defensive movements (Escape!)

After all Defenses:

- Follow agency policies and procedures in regard to self-defense.

- Report and Document immediately.

Outside Block Defense

It is a technique that teaches individuals how to deflect an imminent assault to either side of their body.

Objective—Demonstrate how to properly use a defensive outside block against a physical assault coming to either side of your body.

Performance—Outside Block Defense

1. Assume the bladed stance.
2. Bring either your right or left (or both) up arms in front of your body and pivot towards the direction of the attack.
3. Your hands can be open or closed.
4. You can use your support arm, strong arm, or both arms to defend against an attack on either side of your body.

During all Defenses:

- Use loud, repetitive defensive verbalizations (NO, STOP, GET BACK, STOP RESISTING, etc.) to direct the aggressor to stop attacking you.

- Use defensive movements (Escape!)

After all Defenses:

- Follow agency policies and procedures in regard to self-defense.

- Report and Document immediately.

Low Block Defense

It is a technique that teaches individuals how to deflect an imminent attack to the lower area of the body.

Objective—Demonstrate how to properly use a low defensive block against a physical assault coming to the lower part of your body.

Performance—Low Block Defense

1. Assume the bladed stance.
2. Bring either your right or left (or both) arm down, sweeping in front of your body and moving the attack away.
3. Your hands can be open or closed.
4. You can use your support arm, strong arm, or both arms to defend against an attack to the lower area of your body.

During all Defenses:

- Use loud, repetitive defensive verbalizations (NO, STOP, GET BACK, STOP RESISTING, etc.) to direct the aggressor to stop attacking you.

- Use defensive movements (Escape!)

After all Defenses:

- Follow agency policies and procedures in regard to self-defense.

- Report and Document immediately.

Module 8: Personal Defense Skills & Techniques

Personal Defensive Techniques Defined

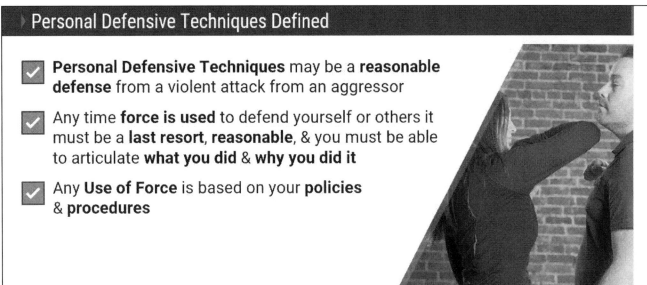

☑ **Personal Defensive Techniques** may be a **reasonable defense** from a violent attack from an aggressor

☑ Any time **force is used** to defend yourself or others it must be a **last resort**, **reasonable**, & you must be able to articulate **what you did** & **why you did it**

☑ Any **Use of Force** is based on your **policies** & **procedures**

Personal Defense Techniques

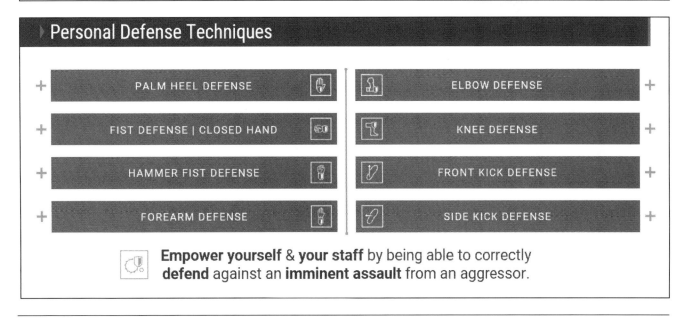

PALM HEEL DEFENSE	ELBOW DEFENSE
FIST DEFENSE | CLOSED HAND	KNEE DEFENSE
HAMMER FIST DEFENSE	FRONT KICK DEFENSE
FOREARM DEFENSE	SIDE KICK DEFENSE

Empower yourself & **your staff** by being able to correctly **defend** against an **imminent assault** from an aggressor.

Palm Heel Defense

The palm heel defense counter technique may be a reasonable defense from a violent attack from an aggressor. Anytime force is used to defend yourself or others. It must be a last resort, reasonable, and you must be able to articulate what you did and why you did it. Any use of force is based on your policies and procedures.

Objective—Demonstrate how to correctly use a palm heel defense technique to defend against an attack from an aggressor.

Performance—Palm Heel Defense
1. Assume the bladed stance.
2. Position your strong or support hand with your heel extended outward.
3. Fingers are in a claw position and have nothing to do with the defense.
4. You can pivot your body forward, thrusting your heel into the desired area of impact.

During all Defenses:
- Use loud, repetitive defensive verbalizations (NO, STOP, GET BACK, STOP RESISTING, etc.) to direct the aggressor to stop attacking you.
- Use defensive movements (Escape!)

After all Defenses:
- Follow agency policies and procedures in regard to self-defense.
- Report and Document immediately.

Fist Defense (Closed Hand)

The fist defense counter technique may be a reasonable defense from a violent attack from an aggressor. Any time force is used to defend yourself or others. It must be a last resort, reasonable, and you must be able to articulate what you did and why you did it. Any use of force is based on your policies and procedures.

Objective—Demonstrate how to correctly use a fist defense technique to defend against an attack from an aggressor.

Performance—Fist Defense (Closed Hand)

1. Assume the bladed stance.

2. Position your strong or support hand with your fingers clenched tightly into your palm.

3. Vertical or horizontal fist positions can be used.

4. You can pivot your body forward, thrusting your fist into the desired area of impact.

Caution: Proper fist position is required to avoid injuring yourself.

During all Defenses:

- Use loud, repetitive defensive verbalizations (NO, STOP, GET BACK, STOP RESISTING, etc.) to direct the aggressor to stop attacking you.
- Use defensive movements (Escape!)

After all Defenses:

- Follow agency policies and procedures in regard to self-defense.
- Report and Document immediately.

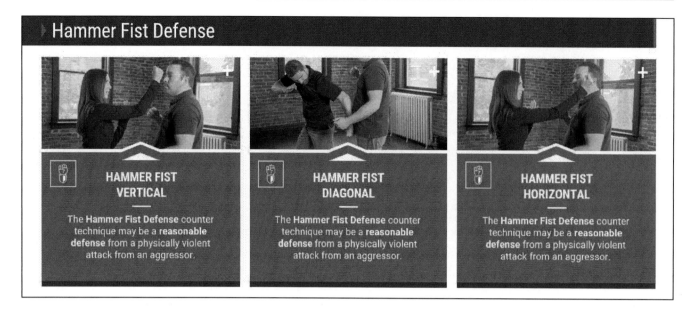

Hammer Fist Defense

The hammer fist defense counter technique may be a reasonable defense from a violent attack from an aggressor. Any time force is used to defend yourself or others. It must be a last resort, reasonable, and you must be able to articulate what you did and why you did it. Any use of force is based on your policies and procedures.

Objective—Demonstrate how to correctly use a fist defense technique to defend against an attack from an aggressor.

Performance—Hammer Fist Defense

1. Assume the bladed stance.

2. Position your strong or support hand with your fingers clenched tightly into your palm.

3. Vertical, diagonal, or horizontal hammer fist defenses may be used.

4. You can pivot your body forward, thrusting your fist into the desired area of impact.

Caution: Proper fist position is required to avoid injuring yourself.

During all Defenses:

- Use loud, repetitive defensive verbalizations (NO, STOP, GET BACK, STOP RESISTING, etc.) to direct the aggressor to stop attacking you.
- Use defensive movements (Escape!)

After all Defenses:

- Follow agency policies and procedures in regard to self-defense.
- Report and Document immediately.

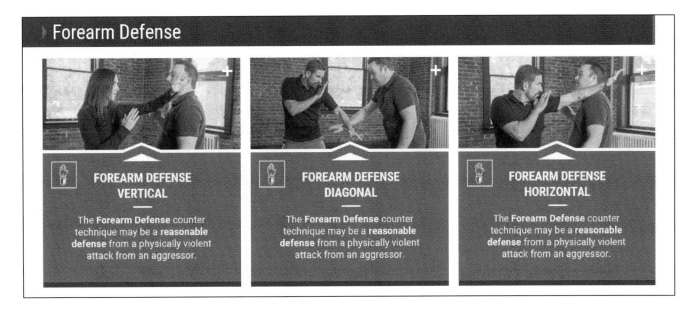

Forearm Defense

The forearm defense counter technique may be a reasonable defense from a violent attack from an aggressor. Anytime force is used to defend yourself or others. It must be a last resort, reasonable, and you must be able to articulate what you did and why you did it. Any use of force is based on your policies and procedures.

Objective—Demonstrate how to correctly use a forearm defense technique to defend against an attack from an aggressor.

Performance—Forearm Defense

1. Assume the bladed stance.

2. Position your strong or support hand with your fingers clenched tightly or in an open position.

3. Vertical, diagonal, or horizontal forearm defenses may be used.

4. You can pivot your body forward or backward, thrusting your forearm into the desired area of impact.

During all Defenses:

- Use loud, repetitive defensive verbalizations (NO, STOP, GET BACK, STOP RESISTING, etc.) to direct the aggressor to stop attacking you.
- Use defensive movements (Escape!)

After all Defenses:

- Follow agency policies and procedures in regard to self-defense.
- Report and Document immediately.

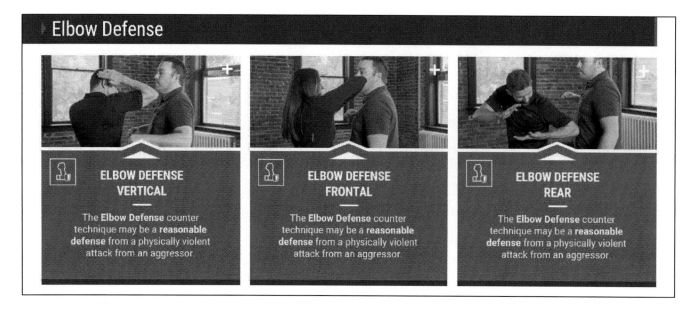

Elbow Defense

The elbow defense counter technique may be a reasonable defense from a violent attack from an aggressor. Anytime force is used to defend yourself or others. It must be a last resort, reasonable, and you must be able to articulate what you did and why you did it. Any use of force is based on your policies and procedures.

Objective—Demonstrate how to correctly use an elbow defense technique to defend against an attack from an aggressor.

Performance—Elbow Defense

1. Assume the bladed stance.
2. When using your strong/support hand elbow, you can blade your hand or clenched hand tightly.
3. Vertical, frontal, and rear elbow defenses may be used.
4. You can pivot your body forward or backward, thrusting your elbow into the desired area of impact.

During all Defenses:

- Use loud, repetitive defensive verbalizations (NO, STOP, GET BACK, STOP RESISTING, etc.) to direct the aggressor to stop attacking you.
- Use defensive movements (Escape!)

After all Defenses:

- Follow agency policies and procedures in regard to self-defense.
- Report and Document immediately.

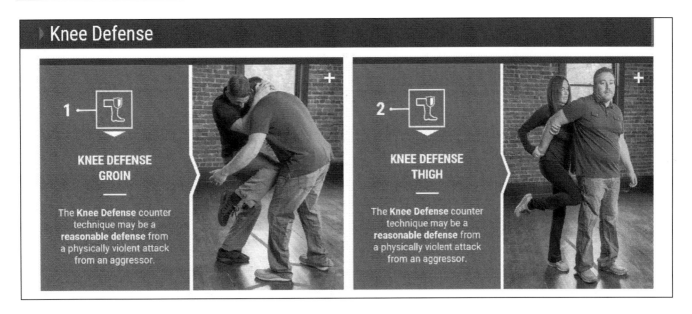

Knee Defense

The knee defense counter technique may be a reasonable defense from a violent attack from an aggressor. Any time force is used to defend yourself or others. It must be a last resort, reasonable, and you must be able to articulate what you did and why you did it. Any use of force is based on your policies and procedures.

Objective—Demonstrate how to correctly use a knee defense technique to defend against an attack from an aggressor.

Performance—Knee Defense

1. Assume the bladed stance.
2. Your support or strong knee can be used.
3. Your foot should be pulled back when defending, creating a pointed knee for impact.
4. You can pivot your body forward, thrusting your knee into the desired area of impact.

Caution: Balance may be compromised when deploying a defensive knee.

During all Defenses:

- Use loud, repetitive defensive verbalizations (NO, STOP, GET BACK, STOP RESISTING, etc.) to direct the aggressor to stop attacking you.
- Use defensive movements (Escape!)

After all Defenses:

- Follow agency policies and procedures in regard to self-defense.
- Report and Document immediately.

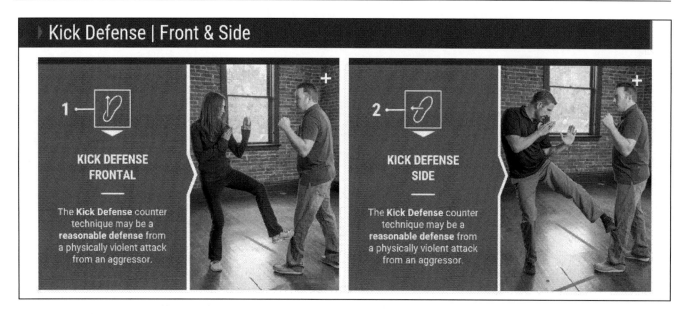

Kick Defense

The kick defense counter technique may be a reasonable defense from a violent attack from an aggressor. Any time force is used to defend yourself or others. It must be a last resort, reasonable, and you must be able to articulate what you did and why you did it. Any use of force is based on your policies and procedures.

Objective—Demonstrate how to correctly use a frontal and sidekick defense technique to defend against an attack from an aggressor.

Performance—Frontal and Side Kick Defense

1. Assume the bladed stance.

2. Your support or strong side can be used for frontal and sidekicks.

3. For the frontal kick, your toes should be pulled back.

4. For the sidekick, use the edge of your outer foot.

Caution: Balance may be compromised when deploying a defensive kick.

During all Defenses:

- Use loud, repetitive defensive verbalizations (NO, STOP, GET BACK, STOP RESISTING, etc.) to direct the aggressor to stop attacking you.
- Use defensive movements (Escape!)

After all Defenses:

- Follow agency policies and procedures in regard to self-defense.
- Report and Document immediately.

Module 9: Weapon Retention Techniques

Holster Weapon Retention | Elbow Weapon Retention

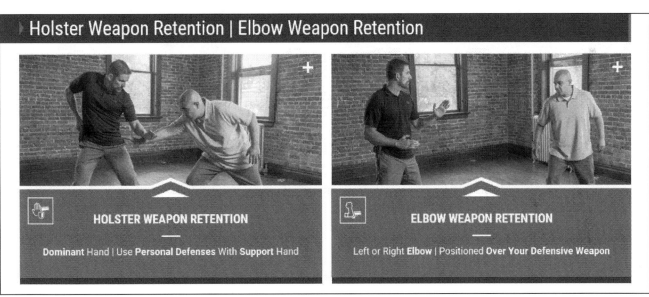

HOLSTER WEAPON RETENTION

Dominant Hand | Use Personal Defenses With Support Hand

ELBOW WEAPON RETENTION

Left or Right Elbow | Positioned Over Your Defensive Weapon

Single Hand Weapon Retention | Two Hand Weapon Retention

SINGLE HAND WEAPON RETENTION

Dominant Hand | Use Personal Defenses With Support Hand

TWO HAND WEAPON RETENTION

Both Hands | Positioned Over Your Defensive Weapon

Holstered Weapon Retention & Elbow, Single Hand, and Two Hand Weapon Retention

Holstered weapon retention is the understanding of your personal equipment and the defensive skills that may be used to keep your weapon holstered. The officer's elbows and hands may be used to assist the officer in retaining his/her personal weapon.

Objective—Demonstrate how to correctly retain your weapon in its holster while using personal defensive skills and movements. Demonstrate how to effectively retain your personal weapon using your elbows and hands.

Performance—Holstered Weapon Retention

1. Assume the bladed stance.

2. Familiarize yourself with your personal holster and its function.

3. Practice personal defensive skills and movements while retaining personal weapons.

4. Position your elbow, single hand (usually strong), or both hands over your personal defensive weapon.

5. Personal defensive skills and movements may be used for retaining personal weapons.

Weapon retention may be used for any personal defensive weapon an officer carries (firearm, chemical sprays, baton, Taser®, etc.)

During all Defenses:

- Use loud, repetitive defensive verbalizations (NO, STOP, GET BACK, STOP RESISTING, etc.) to direct the aggressor to stop attacking you.

- Use defensive movements (Escape if needed)

After all Defenses:

- Follow agency policies and procedures in regard to arrest and control.

- Report and Document immediately.

Module 10: Post-Incident Response and Documentation

Post-Incident Response

It's vital for all employers to have a **Post Incident Response** protocol. The following points are guidelines for the proper and most efficient response to a violent incident.

1	**Triage** | Medical & Hazmat
2	**Report** the incident
3	**Consider all involved** | Staff, Guests, Visitors
4	**Provide for incident debriefing** | CISD & EAP
5	**Document incident** | Follow-up investigations
6	**Initiate corrective actions** to prevent incident reoccurrences

Triage (Medical/Hazmat): Triage is the process of determining the priority of patients' or victims' treatments based on the severity of their condition. Initial first-aid treatment and protocols for hazardous materials and clean-up should be handled immediately.

Report to the Incident: Police, Security, Risk Management, Human Resources, etc. Follow standard operating procedures in reporting incidents.

Consider All Involved—staff, guests, visitors, patients, or anyone who was witness to the incident should be treated accordingly for medical and stress debriefing.

Provide for Incident Debriefing: Debriefing allows those involved with the incident to process the event and reflect on its impact. Depending on the situation, a thorough debriefing may need to take place. Even those not specifically involved in an incident may suffer emotional and psychological trauma.

Critical Incident Stress Debriefing (CISD): is a specific technique designed to assist others in dealing with physical or psychological symptoms that are generally associated with critical incident trauma exposure. Research on the effectiveness of critical incident debriefing techniques has demonstrated that individuals who are provided critical stress debriefing within a 24- to 72-hour window after experiencing the critical incident have lower levels of short- and long-term crisis reactions and psychological trauma.

Employee Assistance Programs (EAP): EAPs are intended to help employees deal with work or personal problems that might adversely impact their work performance, health, and well-being. EAPs generally include assessment, short-term counseling, and referral services for employees and their household members. Employee benefit programs offered by many employers, typically in conjunction with health insurance plans, provide for payment for EAPs.

Document Incident to Include Any Follow-Up Investigations: Post-incident documentation is absolutely critical for reducing liability risk, preventing recurrences, and assisting in follow-up investigations.

Initiate Corrective Actions to Prevent Recurrences: Preventing similar future incidents involves taking proactive corrective actions. Agency management, supervision, security, risk management, employee safety committees, the environment of care committee, etc., should initiate, track, and follow up on corrective actions.

Post-Incident Documentation

1. **Who | What | Where | When | Why | How**
2. **Witnesses** | Who was there?
3. **Narrative** characteristics
4. **Before | During | After**
5. **1st Person | 3rd Person**
6. **Post follow-up** | Track & Trend
7. Follow standard **Operating Procedures**

- **Who–What–Where–When–Why–How:** The first rule in post-incident documentation is the "who, what, where, when, why, and how" rule of reporting. After writing an incident narrative, double-check to see if you have included the first rule of reporting.

- **Witnesses (Who Was There?):** Make sure to include anyone who was a witness to the incident. Staff, visitors, guests, and support services (police, fire, EMS, etc.) can be valuable witnesses should an incident be litigated.

- **Narrative Characteristics:** A proper narrative should describe in detail the characteristics of the violent offender/predator.

- **Before, During, and After:** A thorough incident report will describe what happened before, during, and after the incident. Details matter!

- **1st Person vs. 3rd Person:** The account of an incident can be described in the first person or the third person. This can be specific to your agency's protocols or the preference of the person documenting the incident.

- **Post-Follow-Up (Track and Trend):** Most agencies use electronic documentation, which allows for easy retrieval, tracking, and trending. Using technology assists agencies in following up and initiating proactive corrections.

- **Follow Standard Operating Procedures:** Whether handwriting incident reports or using electronic documentation and charting, staff should consistently and thoroughly document all incidents relating to violence in the workplace.

Elements of Reporting Force/Self-Defense

Report and Document: After any situation involving the defense of yourself or another person, proper documentation and reporting are crucial. The events of the assault or attempted assault should be reported to security/police. The police/security will document the incident and start an investigation. You should also document the account for your own internal records. This can protect you in a possible legal situation that could arise out of using force to defend yourself. As you document your account of the incident, make sure to report to security/police any details you missed during your initial report to them.

What type of force/self-defense/technique was used during the incident?

Be specific in your documentation regarding the type of control, defense, and force that was used during the incident.

How long did the incident and resistance last?

Important to note the length of the resistance, as this is a factor relative to exhaustion and increasing the level of force.

Was any de-escalation used?

Verbal and non-verbal de-escalation techniques should be noted.

Were you in fear of injury (bodily harm) to yourself, others, or the subject?

Fear is a distressing emotion aroused by a perceived threat, impending danger, evil, or pain.

If so, Why?

Fear is a basic survival mechanism occurring in response to a specific stimulus, such as pain or the threat of danger.

Thoroughly explain, and make sure to document completely.

The importance of documentation cannot be overemphasized. Documentation ensures proper training standards are met, policies and procedures are understood, certification standards are met, liability and risk management mitigation, and departmental and organizational requirements are maintained.

Special Note: Every person must take into consideration their moral, legal, and ethical beliefs, rights, and understandings when using any type of force to defend themselves or others. Personal Safety Training Inc. makes no legal declaration, representation, or claim as to what force should be used or not used during a self-defense/assault incident or situation. Each trainee must take into consideration their ability, agency policies and procedures, and state and federal laws.

AVADE® DTS™ Training Review

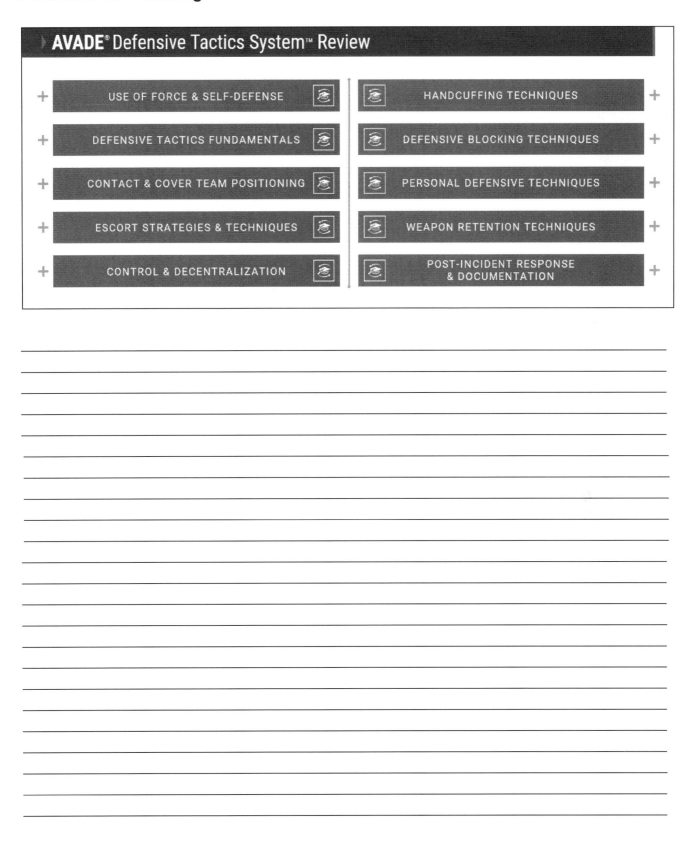

About the Author

David Fowler is the founder and president of (PSTI) Personal Safety Training Incorporated and AVADE® Training, located in Coeur d'Alene, ID. He is responsible for the overall management and operations of PSTI and AVADE®, which offers seminars, training, consulting, and protective details. Since 1990, David has been involved in security operations, training, and protective details.

He is the author of the SOCS® (Security Oriented Customer Service) program and training manual, as well as the AVADE® Personal Safety Training and Workplace Violence Prevention programs and training manuals. He is also the author of the book *Be Safe Not Sorry - The art and science of keeping YOU and your family safe from crime and violence*. David has worked with thousands of individuals and hundreds of agencies and corporations throughout the United States and Canada. His presentations have included international, national, and local seminars. David's thorough understanding of safety and security and martial science adds an exciting and interesting approach to his style of presentation.

David is a certified master instructor in several nationally recognized training programs such as Workplace Violence Prevention (AVADE®), Pepper Spray Defense™, Handcuffing Tactics™, Security Oriented Customer Service (SOCS®), Defensive Tactics System™ (DTS™), Defense Baton™, Security Incident Reporting System™ (SIRS™) and AVADE® Personal Safety Training. David has certified and trained thousands of individuals in these programs and others throughout the United States and abroad.

He is a graduate of (ESI) Executive Security International's Advanced Executive Protection Program and the Protective Intelligence and Investigations program. He is also a member of ASIS (American Society for Industrial Security), The International Law Enforcement Educators & Trainers Association (ILEETA), and the International Association of Healthcare Safety & Security (IAHSS).

David brings insight, experience, and a passion for empowering people and organizations utilizing the training programs and protective services that he offers here in the United States and in other countries. He is considered by many to be the most dynamic and motivational speaker and trainer in the security and personal safety industry.

David is happily married to the love of his life, Genelle Fowler. They live in Coeur d' Alene, ID, and have five children and three grandchildren. David and Genelle have committed their lives to serve others through the mission of safety. Both David and Genelle travel extensively, providing training and consulting to corporations throughout North America.

Bibliography, Reference Guide, and Recommended Reading

Books, CD's, DVD's and Websites

Adams, Terry, and Rob. *Seminar Production Business: Your Step by Step Guide to Success.* Entrepreneur Press, Canada 2003.

Albrecht, Steve. *Surviving Street Patrol: The Officer's Guide to Safe and Effective Policing.* Paladin Press, Boulder, CO 2001.

Amdur, Ellis. *Dueling with O-sensei: Grappling with the Myth of the Warrior Sage.* Edgework, Seattle, WA 2000.

Andersen, Peter A. *The Complete Idiot's Guide to Body Language.* Alpha Books, Indianapolis, IN 2004.

Andrews, Andy. *The Travelers Gift: Seven Decisions that Determine Personal Success.* Nelsen Books, Nashville, Tennessee, 2002.

Arapakis, Maria. *Soft Power: How to Speak Up, Set Limits, and Say No Without Losing Your Lover, Your Job, or Your Friends.* Warner Books, Inc. NY, NY, 1990.

Artwhohl, Alexis & Christensen, Loren. *Deadly Force Encounters: What Cops need to know to mentally and physically prepare for and survive a gunfight.* Paladin Press, Boulder, CO 1997.

ASIS International. *Security Management Magazine.* www.securitymanagment.com 2006-2016.

Branca, Andrew. The Law of SELF-DEFENSE: The indispensable Guide for the Armed Citizen. Law of Self Defense, Maynard, MA 2016

Brown, Tom. *Survival Guides: Americas Bestselling Wilderness Series.* Berkley Books, New York, 1984.

Byrnes, John D. *Before Conflict: Preventing Aggressive Behavior.* Scarecrow Press, Lanham, Maryland and Oxford 2002.

Canfield, Jack and Bunch, Jim. *The Ultimate Life Workshop: 7 Strategies for Creating the Ultimate Life.* Live Workshop - February 2008.

Carnegie, Dale. *Golden Book*. www.dalecarnegie.com

Carnegie, Dale. *How to Win Friends & Influence People*. Pocket Books, NY, NY 1936.

Chodron, Thubten. *Working With Anger*. Snow Lion Publication, Ithaca, NY 2001.

Christenson, Loren. *DEFENSIVE TACTICS: Modern Arrest & Control Techniques for Today's Police Warrior.* Turtle Press, Washington, DC 2008

Christenson, Loren. *Fighting in the Clinch: Vicious Strikes, Street Wrestling, and Gouges for Real Fights.* Paladin Press, Boulder, CO 2009

Christensen, Loren. *The Way Alone: Your Path to Excellence in the Martial Arts.* Paladin Press, Boulder, CO 1987.

Christensen, Loren. *Warriors: On Living with Courage, Discipline, and Honor*. Paladin Press, Boulder, CO 2004.

Covey, Stephen R. *The 7 Habits of Highly Effective People: Powerful Lessons in Personal Change*. Fireside, NY, NY 1989.

Covey, Stephen R. *The 8th Habit: From Effectiveness to Greatness*. Better Life Media, DVD and CD, 2004.

Day Laura, *Practical Intuition*. Villard Books, NY, NY 1996

DeBecker, Gavin. *The Gift of Fear*. Dell Publishing, NY, NY 1997.

DeBecker, Gavin. *Fear Less: Real Truth about Risk, Safety, and Security in a Time of Terrorism.* Little Brown and Company, Boston, NY, London 2002.

DeBecker, Gavin & Taylor, Tom & Marquart, Jeff. *Just 2 Seconds: Using Time and Space To Defeat Assassins.* The Gavin DeBecker Center for the Study and Reduction of Violence, a not-for-profit foundation, Studio City, CA 2008.

DeBecker, Gavin. *Protecting the Gift: Keeping Children and Teenagers Safe (and Parents Sane)*. A Dell Trade Paperback, NY, NY 1999.

Deshimaru, Taisen. *The Zen Way to the Martial Arts: A Japanese Master Reveals the Secrets of the Samurai*. Penguin Compass. NY, NY, 1982.

DeMasco, Steve. *The Shaolin Way: 10 Modern Secrets of Survival from a Shaolin Kung Fu Grandmaster.* Harper, NY, NY 2006.

Divine, Mark. *The WAY of the SEAL: Think Like an Elite Warrior to Lead and Succeed.* Readers Digest, White Plains, NY 2013

Dyer, Wayne. *The Power of Intention; Learning to Co-Create your world your way.* Hay House, CA, 2004.

Eckman, Paul. *Emotions Revealed: Recognizing Faces and Feelings to Improve Communication and Emotional Life*: Henry Holt & Company, NY, NY, 2007.

Eckman, Paul. *Telling Lies.* WW. Norton Company, NY, and London. 1991.

Eggerichs, Emerson. *Love & Respect: The Love She Most Desires and The respect he Desperately Needs.* Gale Cengage Learning. US 2010

Fowler, David. *Be Safe Not Sorry, the Art and Science of keeping YOU and your family Safe from Crime and Violence.* Personal Safety Training, Inc. Coeur d Alene, ID 2011.

Fowler, David. *Violence In The Workplace: Education, Prevention & Mitigation.* Personal Safety Training, Inc. Coeur d Alene, ID 2012.

Fowler, David. *To Serve and Protect: Providing SERVICE while maintaining SAFETY in the Workplace.* Personal Safety Training, Inc. Coeur d Alene, ID 2015

Fowler, David. SURVIVE an Active Shooter: Awareness, Preparedness, and Response for EXTREME VIOLENCE. Personal Safety Training, Inc. Coeur d Alene, ID 2016

Funakoshi, Gichin. *Karate-Do My Way of Life.* Kodansha International, Tokyo, NY. London, 1975.

Funakoshi, Gichin. The Twenty Guiding Principles of Karate. Kodansha International, Tokyo, NY. London, 2012

Gallo, Carmine. *Inspire Your Audience: 7 Keys to Influential Presentations*. Paper. Communication Skills Coach – Author of Fire Them Up!

Gallups, Carl. Be Though Prepared: Equipping the Church for Persecution and Times of Trouble. WND Books. 2015

Gardner, Daniel. *The Science of Fear: How the Culture of Fear MANIPULATES YOUR BRAIN.* Penguin Books Ltd, Strand, London 2009

Garner, Bryan. *Black's Law Dictionary: Seventh Edition*. West Group, St. Paul, MN, 1999.

Gladwell, Malcolm. *Blink*. Little, Brown & Company, NY 2005.

Glennon, Jim. *Arresting Communication: Essential Interaction Skills for Law Enforcement*. LifeLine Training & Caliber Press, Elmhurst, IL 2010.

Goleman, Daniel. *Emotional Intelligence*. Bantam Books, NY, NY 2005.

Gray, John. *Beyond Mars and Venus*. Better Life Media, DVD and CD, 2004.

Gregory, Hamilton. *Public Speaking for College and Career: Fifth Edition*. McGraw-Hill, Boston, 1999.

Gross, Linden. *Surviving A Stalker: Everything you need to know to keep yourself safe*. Marlowe and Company, NY, NY, 2000.

Grossman, Dave & Christensen, Loren. *On Combat: The Psychology of Deadly Conflict in War and Peace*. PPCT Research, IL, 2004.

Grossman, Dave & DeGaetano, Gloria. *Stop Teaching our Kids to Kill: A call to action against TV, Movie & Video Game Violence*. Crown Publishers, NY, NY 1999.

Harrell, Keith. *Attitude is Everything: 10 Life-Changing Steps to Turning Attitude Into Action*. Harper Collins Publishing, NY, NY 1999.

Hawkins, David R, MD. *Power vs. Force: The Hidden Determinants of Human Behavior*. Veritas, Sedona, AZ, 2004.

Headley, Steve. *Assault Prevention Workshop*. Assault Prevention Workshops, LLC, 2009.

Hyams, Joe. *Zen in the Martial Arts*. Bantam Books, Toronto, NY, London, Sydney, Auckland, 1982.

IAHSS. *Basic Training Manual and Study Guide for Healthcare Security Officers*. Lombard, IL, 1995.

IAHSS. *Journal of Healthcare Protection Management*. Bayside, NY 2008-2016.

Jo-Ellan Dimitrius, Ph.D., and Mark Mazzarella. *Reading People: How to Understand People and Predict their Behavior-Anytime, Anyplace*. Ballantine Books, NY, NY 1999.

Kane, Lawrence A. *Surviving Armed Assaults*. YMAA Publication Center, Boston, MA, 2006.

Kinnaird, Brian. *Use of Force: Expert Guidance for Decisive Force Response*. Looseleaf Law Publications, Flushing, NY 2003.

Krebs & Henry & Gabriele. *When Violence Erupts: A Survival Guide for Emergency Responders.* The C.V. Mosby Company, St. Louis, Baltimore, Philadelphia, Toronto, 1990.

Lamnier, Sandra. Workplace Violence: Before, During, and After. ASIS International 2003

Larkin, Tim, and Ranck-Buhr, Chris. *How to Survive The Most Critical 5 Seconds of Your Life.* The TFT Group. Sequim, WA 2008

Larkin, Tim. When Violence is the Answer: Learning how to do what it takes when your life is at stake. Little, Brown and Company, NY, NY 2017

Lawler, Jennifer. *Dojo Wisdom: 100 Simple Ways to Become a Stronger, Calmer, more Courageous Person.* Penguin Compass, NY, NY 2003.

Leaf, Caroline. *Switch on your Brain: The Key to Peak Happiness, Thinking, and Health.* Baker Books, Grand Rapids, MI 2013

Lee, Bruce. *Tao of Jeet Kune Do*. Ohara Publications, Santa Clarita, CA 1975.

Lee, Johnny. *Addressing Domestic Violence in the Workplace*. HRD Press, Inc. Amherst, MA 2005

Lee, Linda. *The Bruce Lee Story*. Ohara Publications, Santa Clarita, CA 1989.

Lion, John, MD. *Evaluation and Management of the Violent Patient: Guidelines in the Hospital and Institution*. Charles C. Thomas Publisher, Springfield, IL 1972.

Little, John. *The Warrior Within The philosophies of Bruce Lee to better understand the world around you and achieve a rewarding life*. Contemporary Books, Chicago, IL 1996.

Loehr, James, and Migdwo, Jeffrey. Breathe In Breathe Out: Inhale Energy and Exhale Stress By Guiding and Controlling Your Breathing. Time-Life Books, Alexandria, VI 1986

Lorenz, Conrad. *On Aggression*. MJF Book. NY 1963

Machowicz, Richard J. *Unleash The Warrior Within: Develop the Focus, Discipline, Confidence, and Courage You Need to Achieve Unlimited Goals.* Marlowe & Company, NY, 2002.

Mackay, Harvey. "Harvey Mackay's Column This Week." Weekly e-mail publication, www.harveymackay.com

MacYoung, Marc "Animal." *Ending Violence Quickly: How Bouncers, Bodyguards, and Other Security Professionals Handle Ugly Situations.* Paladin Press, Boulder, CO 1993.

Maggio, Rosalie. *How to Say It: Choice Words, Phrases, Sentences, and Paragraphs for Every Situation*. Prentice-Hall Press, NY, NY 2001.

Maltz, Maxwell, MD. *Psycho-Cybernetics: A New Way to Get More Living Out Of Life.* Essandress, NY, NY 1960.

Marcinko, Richard. *The Rogue Warriors Strategy For Success*. Pocket Books, NY, NY 1997.

Mason, Tom & Chandley Mark. *Managing Violence and Aggression: A Manual for Nurses and Health Care Workers.* Churchill Livingstone, Edinburgh, 1999.

McGrew, James. *Think Safe: Practical Measures to Increase Security at Home, at Work, and Throughout Life.* Cameo Publications, Hilton Head Island, SC, 2004.

McTaggart, Lynne. *The Intention Experiment: Using Your Thoughts to Change Your Life and the World.* Free Press, NY, NY 2007.

Medina, John. *Brain Rules: 12 Principles for Surviving and Thriving at Work, Home, and School.* Pear Press, Seattle, WA 2008.

Miller, Rory. *FACING VIOLENCE: Preparing for the Unexpected-Ethically, Emotionally, Physically, Without Going to Prison.* YMAA Publication Center, Wolfeboro, NH 2011

Miller, Rory. Training For Sudden Violence. 72 Practical Drills. Publication Center, Wolfeboro, NH 2016

Murphy, Joseph, Dr. *The Power of Your Subconscious Mind.* Bantam Books, NY, Toronto, London, Sidney, Auckland 2000.

Musashi, Miyamoto. Translated by Thomas Cleary. *The Book of Five Rings.* Shambala, Boston, and London 2003.

Norris, Chuck. *The Secret Power Within: Zen Solutions to Real Problems.* Broadway Books, NY 1996.

Norris, Chuck. *Winning Tournament Karate*. Ohara Publications, Burbank, CA 1975.

Nowicki, Ed. *Total Survival.* Performance Dimensions, Powers Lake, MI 1993.

Omartian, Stormie. *PRAYER WARRIOR: The Power of Praying Your Wat to Victory.* Harvest House Publishers, Eugene, OR 2013

Ouellette, Roland W. *Management of Aggressive Behavior.* Performance Dimension Publishing, Powers Lake, WI 1993.

Palumbo, Dennis. *The Secrets of Hakkoryu Jujutsu: Shodan Tactics.* Paladin Press Boulder, CO 1987.

Parker, S.L. *212, the extra degree.* The Walk the Talk Co. 2005 www.walkthetalk.com.

Patire, Tom. *Tom Patire's Personal Protection Handbook.* Three Rivers Press, NY 2003.

Peale, Norman Vincent. *Six Attitudes for Winners.* Tyndale House Publishers, Inc. Wheaton, Il, 1989.

Peale, Norman Vincent. *The Power of Positive Thinking.* Ballantine Books, NY, NY 1956.

Pease, Allan, and Barbara. *The Definitive Book of Body Language.* Bantam Dell. NY, NY, 2004.

Perkins, John & Ridenhour, Al & Kovsky Matt. *Attack Proof: The Ultimate Guide to Personal Protection.* Human Kinetics, Champaign, IL, 2000.

Pietsch, William. *HUMAN BE-ING: How to have a creative relationship instead of a power struggle.* Lawrence Hill & Company Publishers Inc, NY, NY 1974

PPCT Management Systems, Inc. *Defensive Tactics Instructor Manual.* PPCT 2005.

Purpura, Philip. *The Security Handbook: Second Edition.* Butterworth Heinemann, Boston, 2003.

Rail, Robert R. *The Unspoken Dialogue: Understanding Body Language and Controlling Interviews and Negotiations.* Varro Press, Kansas City 2001.

Ralston, Peter. *Cheng Hsin: The Principles of Effortless Power.* North Atlantic Books, Berkeley, CA 1989.

Ratey, John J. *Spark: The Revolutionary New Science of Exercise and the Brain.* Little, Brown and Co., NY, NY 2008.

Rawls, Neal. *BE ALERT BE AWARE HAVE A PLAN: The complete guide to protecting yourself, your home, your family.* Globe Pequot Press, Guilford, CT

Rodale Inc. *Men's Health Today, 2007.* Rodale Inc. US 2007.

Sandford, John, and Paula. *The Transformation of the Inner Man.* Bridge Publishing, Inc. S. Plainfield, NJ 1982

Strong, Sanford. *Strong on Defense: Survival Rules to Protect You and Your Family from Crime.* Pocket Books, NY, NY 1996.

Sjodin, Terri. New Sales Speak: *The 9 Biggest Sales Presentation Mistakes and How to Avoid Them.* Better Life Media. DVD and CD 2004.

Soo, Chee, *The Chinese Art of T'ai Chi Ch'uan: The Taoist way to mental and physical health*. The Aquarian Press, Wellingborough, Northamptonshire 1984.

Staley, Charles. *The Science of Martial Arts Training.* Multi-Media Books, Burbank, CA 1999.

Tarani, Steve. Prefense The 90% Advantage: Preventing Bad Things from Happening to Good People. Tarani, US, 2014

The Evidence Bible, NKJV, Bridge-Logos Publishers- © 2011 by Ray Comfort. Alachua, FL.

The Results Driven Manager. *Dealing with Difficult People*. Harvard Business School Publishing Corp, Boston, MA 2005.

Theriault, Jean Yves. *Full Contact Karate.* Contemporary Books, Inc. Chicago, 1983.

The World's Greatest Treasury of Health Secrets. Bottom Line Publications, Stamford, CT 2006.

Thompson, George. *Verbal Judo*. Quill William Morrow, NY 1993.

Tsunetomo, Yamamoto. *Hagakure: The Book of the Samurai.* Kodansha International, Tokyo, NY, London 1979.

Turner, James T. *Violence in the Medical Care Setting*. Aspen Systems Corporation, Rockville, MD 1984.

Tzu, Sun. *The Art of War*. Samuel Griffith Interpretation, Oxford University Press, 1993.

Ueshiba, Kisshomaru. *The Spirit of Aikido*. Kodansha International, Tokyo, NY, London, 1987.

Van Horne, Patrick, and Riley, Jason. *LEFT of BANG: How the Marine Corps' Combat Hunter Program Can Save Your Life*. Black Irish Entertainment LLC, NY and Los Angeles, 2014

US Dept. of Justice. *Workplace Violence: Issues in Response.* Critical Incident Response Group, National Center for the Analysis of Violent Crime, FBI Academy, Quantico, Virginia 2001.

Wallace, Bill. *The Ultimate Kick: The Wallace Method to Winning Karate.* Unique Publications, Burbank, CA, 1987.

Wagner, Pellegrini, Kanarek, Ryan, Janich, McCann. The Ultimate Guide to Reality-Based Self-Defense. Black Belt Books, South Korea 2010

Webster, Noah. *Webster's Dictionary*. Modern Promotions/Publishers, NY, NY 1984.

Willis, Brian. *W.I.N. 2: Insights Into Training and Leading Warriors.* Warrior Spirit Books, Calgary, Alberta, Canada 2009.

Websites and Weblinks

http://www.AVADEtraining.com

http://www.personalsafetytraining.com

http://www.socstraining.com

http://www.tribalsecuritytraining.com

http://www.wpvprevention.com

http://www.aaets.org/article54.htm

http://en.wikipedia.org/wiki/Excited_delirium

http://en.wikipedia.org/wiki/Chemical_restraint

http://en.wikipedia.org/wiki/Positional_asphyxia

AVADE® TRAINING COURSES
FOR YOU & YOUR AGENCY

▶ Personal Safety Training Inc. | AVADE® Training Programs

The only way to deal with conflict and avoid violence of any type is through *awareness, vigilance, avoidance, defensive training, and escape planning.*

David Fowler, President of Personal Safety Training Inc., specializes in nationally recognized training programs that *empower individuals, increase confidence, and promote pro-active preventative solutions.*

OSHA, Labor & Industries, Joint Commission, State WPV Laws, and the Department of Health all recognize that programs like PSTI's are *excellent preventive measures to reduce crime, violence, and aggression in the workplace.*

Personal Safety Training Inc. is committed to providing the finest level of training and service to you and your employees. Whether you are an individual or represent an agency, we have the Basic and Instructor Course Certifications that you need.

▶ Training Options

PSTI | AVADE® Offers Multiple Training Options for Your Organization:

☑ **On-Site Training** (We will come to you!)
No need to send staff away for training. PSTI will come to your place of business and train your staff.

☑ **Train-the-Trainer** (Instructor Seminars)
The most cost-effective way to implement PSTI Training courses for your organization. We can come to you for instructor courses or you can send staff to one of our upcoming seminars.

☑ **Combo Classes**
Combination classes are where Basic Training and Instructor Training are combined during on-site training. It is a great way to introduce PSTI Training with our initial instruction and then continue on with your own instructors.

☑ **E-Learning**
Are you looking for a training solution to integrate a Workplace Violence Prevention Program in order to meet compliance standards for both State and Federal guidelines? The AVADE® E-Learning programs offer a great solution to give your staff an introductory yet comprehensive training program that can be completed as needed.

☑ **Course Duration Options**
PSTI offers multiple options and course durations from introductory to advanced training. Course lengths range from: 2-hr. Introductory Courses, 1/2 Day Training Sessions, 1-Day Classes, 2-Day Classes, and Train the Trainer (Instructor Classes)

CONTACT US TODAY!
Personal Safety Training Inc. | AVADE® Training
P.O. Box 2957 Coeur d'Alene, ID 83816
Phone: 208-664-5551 | Fax: 208-664-5556 | Email: info@personalsafetytraining.com
personalsafetytraining.com | avadetraining.com

Education, Prevention, and *Mitigation* for *Violence in the Workplace*
© Personal Safety Training Inc. | AVADE® Training

AVADE® TRAINING COURSES
FOR YOU & YOUR AGENCY

> **Training Courses**

AVADE® Training Courses

☑ **AVADE® Workplace Violence Prevention | avadetraining.com**
The AVADE® WPV Training is offered as a Basic and Instructor level course for private corporations, healthcare, security, and agencies wanting to educate, prevent, and mitigate the risk of violence to their employees.

☑ **AVADE® De-Escalation | avadedeescalation.com**
When individuals are in crisis, you are either escalting or de-escalating them. The AVADE® De-Escalation Training is designed to educate, prevent, and mitigate the risk of escalation, aggression, and violence in the workplace.

☑ **AVADE® Active Shooter | avadeactiveshooter.com**
The AVADE® Active Shooter Training is designed to increase awareness, preparedness, and response to extreme violence. The philosopphy of education, prevention, and mitigation is the cornerstone of this training program.

☑ **AVADE® Home Health Care | avadehomehealthcare.com**
The AVADE® Home Health Care Training program is designed to educate, prevent, and mitigate aggression and violence for workers in the Home Health Care and Hospice industry.

☑ **AVADE® DTS™ (Defensive Tactics System) | dts-training.com**
The AVADE® DTS™ Training program covers basic defensive tactics, control techniques, and defensive interventions. This course includes stance, movement, escort techniques, takedowns, defensive blocking, active defense skills, weapon retention, handcuffing, post-incident response and documentation, and more.

☑ **AVADE® HDTS™ (Healthcare Defensive Tactics System) | hdts-training.com**
The AVADE® HDTS™ Training program for healthcare covers basic defensive tactics, control techniques, and defensive interventions. This course includes stance, movement, escort techniques, takedowns, team intervention, defensive blocking, active defense skills, weapon retention, patient restraint techniques, handcuffing, post-incident response and documentation, and more.

☑ **AVADE® Handcuffing Tactics™ | handcuffingtactics.com**
Training in the use of plastic, chain, or hinged handcuffs. standing, kneeling, and prone handcuffing techniques are covered. In this training course you will also learn defensive tactics fundamentals, proper positioning, nomenclature, risk factors, and post-incident response and documentation.

☑ **AVADE® Defense Baton™ | defensebaton.com**
Training in the use of an expandable bat, straight stick, or riot control baton. Techniques and topics in this training include: vulnerable areas of the body, stance, movement, blocks, control holds, counter techniques, draws, and retention techniques.

☑ **AVADE® Pepper Spray Defense™ | pepperspraydefense-training.com**
Tatical and practical concepts of when and how to use pepper spray in a variety of environmental situations. Aerosol pepper is a great less-than-lethal control and defense option for agencies that encounter violence and aggression.

AVADE® TRAINING COURSES
FOR YOU & YOUR AGENCY

☑ **AVADE® SIRS™** (Safety Incident Reporting System) | **sirs-training.com**
The AVADE® SIRS™ Training program teaches staff how to effectively and intelligenty write safety incident reports. Documentation of safety incidents is absolutely cirtical to your agency's ability to track and trend, reduce liability, and share vital information. If you're like most agencies, you know that proper, structured, effective, and reliable reports save time, money, and allow you to track incidents and reduce liability risk.

SOCS® Training Course

☑ **SOCS®** (Safety Oriented Customer Service) | **socstraining.com**
SOCS® Training teaches staff how to identify and provide great customer service while maintaining safety in the workplace. The core concept of the training is to be able to provide excellent service without having to think about it. Creating habits, skills and taking action, for exceptional customer service is the goal of the SOCS® Training program.

Safety Training Books

☑ **AVADE® Personal Safety Training**
Buy the ultimate book and training on how to keep you and your family safe. This training guide is designed to increase your overall safety in all environments. The curriculum is based on David Fowler's book, **Be Safe Not Sorry- The Art and Science of Keeping You and Your Family Safe From Crime and Violence.**

☑ **AVADE® Violence in the Workplace** (Versions I, II, & III)
Purchase the the book on how to be safe in the workplace. This text is based on the AVADE® Training program. Can't come to a class, at least get the book! The knowledge contained in these pages will teach you awareness, vigilance, avoidance, defensive interventions, and escape strategies for your place of business.

▶ AVADE® Training Programs Serves Multiple Industries

Industries: Healthcare | Corporate | Security | Gaming | Churches

HEALTHCARE

CORPORATE

SECURITY

GAMING

CHURCHES

Education, Prevention, and Mitigation for *Violence in the Workplace*

© Personal Safety Training Inc. | AVADE® Training

AVADE® TRAINING COURSES
FOR YOU & YOUR AGENCY

▶ PSTI Training Products

Training Products: Instructor Manuals | Student Guides | Training Weapons

CORPORATE BASIC
DAVID FOWLER

CORPORATE ADVANCED
DAVID FOWLER

HEALTHCARE BASIC
DAVID FOWLER

HEALTHCARE ADVANCED
DAVID FOWLER

DE-ESCALATION
DAVID FOWLER

ACTIVE SHOOTER TRAINING
DAVID FOWLER

DEFENSIVE TACTICS SYSTEM
DAVID FOWLER

HEALTHCARE DEFENSIVE TACTICS SYSTEM
DAVID FOWLER

HANDCUFFING TACTICS
DAVID FOWLER

DEFENSE BATON
DAVID FOWLER

PEPPER SPRAY DEFENSE
DAVID FOWLER

SAFETY INCIDENT REPORTING SYSTEM
DAVID FOWLER

VISIT **PERSONALSAFETYTRAINING.COM** OR
CONTACT US AT **1-866-773-7763** TO LEARN MORE!

Education, Prevention, and Mitigation for *Violence in the Workplace*

® Personal Safety Training Inc. | AVADE® Training

Made in the USA
Monee, IL
01 August 2023

40251170R00066